Lean on Me

CANCER
Through a Carer's Eyes

by

LORRAINE KEMBER

ISBN 0-646-49969-6

**Copies of this book can be obtained by contacting
Author: Lorraine Kember
PO Box 70 Beechboro WA 6063
Email: lorakeet@iinet.net.au**

Part proceeds of each copy sold will be donated to cancer research.

Printed and Bound by Success Print
61-8-9279 3214
7a Goongarrie Street
Bayswater
Western Australia 6053

Typesetting by Color Logic
61-8-9471 1695
19 Hubert Road
Maylands
Western Australia 6051

Cover Photo by Michelle Kember of Brian and Lorraine
Exmouth 1998

It takes courage to truly travel on the road with a loved one facing a terminal illness. Lorraine takes us with her on that journey through the entries in her diary, capturing so graphically, the roller-coaster of emotions experienced by many carers supporting their loved ones through this most difficult time.

It was a privilege to be involved in the care of such a courageous man and to witness the continuous, selfless and loving care which Lorraine maintained throughout their journey together. "Lean on Me" is a very apt title for this story.

To others on a similar journey (or who have already completed theirs), I'm sure this book will bring comfort from the practical advise Lorraine offers from her own experiences, and relief to know that someone else shares their needs and feelings without guilt. Likewise, professional carers involved in Palliative Care will gain useful insight into the depth of despair that carers experience, but are unable to articulate to others as Lorraine does so well to her diary and expresses in her poems.

The feeling of satisfaction and peace which Lorraine obtains from a job well done is richly deserved.

Janet Craven. RN
Palliative Care Nurse
Silver Chain Hospice Care Service

It was with great interest and slight trepidation that I picked up the manuscript for this book. Having known both Lorraine and Brian for several years, and having shared many of the highs and lows that they went through, I was curious as to how the story would look in print. I was also a little worried as if the telling of the tale might lesson it in some way: - All fears allayed.

I believe that this book is truly unique. It combines a thorough, warm, insightful and intelligent description of a very personal journey. After getting to know Brian and Lorraine in a warm introduction to them both, the book takes you through the devastating diagnosis and all of the treatments and problems that they then faced. Lorraine's writing style actually involves you in the book, as though you have known them for years and you feel the same highs and lows that they do. It truly takes you on their journey.

The way that Brian and Lorraine approach the illness and its treatment really provides hope for all who read this book. I have not read another book written by a lay person which so captures the essence of the battle against cancer, which also displays such a thorough understanding of the disease and its complexities.

Lorraine's refreshing discussions, thoughts and views really do provide a good insight to the trials and tribulations that accompany an illness such as this but also emphasise the good things that they experienced together and the benefits they got from their treatment. It is this writing that actually gives such hope to anybody who is potentially facing the same journey.

That this is Lorraine's first attempt at writing, is truly remarkable. Her writing style is brilliant and her book is interspersed with poems which she penned along the way. Her poems are worth a separate publication in themselves.

I believe that this is a truly amazing book that everybody with cancer should read. Any families who have been touched by this disease will undoubtedly find in it inspiration and hope.

DR ANDREW DEAN
MB Ch.B. MRCP (UK).FRACP
Consultant Physician in Palliative Care
Perth, Western Australia

October 2003

Life like a flower in bloom
Sheds its petals day by day
As silently
It fades away

BRIAN

He was only a child when it begun
And he played as children do
In his yard with his toy cars and tip trucks
But his sand was asbestos blue

Brian as a child

Brian was a Wittenoom child. For a short period of seven
months he lived there with his parents, innocently
playing in and inhaling the deadly asbestos dust that lay
around the town and houses. He was seven years old.

CONTENTS

Dedicated to my late husband Brian

Whose unfailing spirit and remarkable courage

remain an inspiration

to us all.

ACKNOWLEDGEMENTS:

I wish to express my thanks to Doctor Hugh Lesley whose wisdom, compassion, and support was greatly appreciated. His advice regarding my anticipatory grief provided the foundation for the strength that held me up throughout the following years.

I also wish to thank Jill Taylor, my counsellor, who listened tirelessly and helped me put things into perspective.

PALLIATIVE CARE TEAM

Dr Andrew Dean and all of the Palliative Care Team had a dramatic impact on our lives. Their invaluable experience and commitment in dealing with the terminally ill, and their knowledge concerning the treatment of associated pain and symptoms, greatly eased our burden. So too, their wisdom, through which they recognised Brian's spirit, and came to know and respect the vital man he was, despite the ravages of his disease. They also came to know me and were always there to listen, support, and comfort me throughout Brian's illness, death, and beyond. They have my eternal gratitude.

SILVER CHAIN

I would like to express my gratefulness to the many Silver Chain Nursing staff I met during Brian's illness. I found them to be friendly, dedicated and compassionate, always present when needed, but never intruding on our privacy; without them we could not have achieved our wish that Brian die at home.

FAMILY

My deepest love and appreciation goes to our children; Michelle, Clint and Julie, for their love and support of their father, and me. Despite their grief they have remained strong, and gone on to achieve remarkable things in their lives. I am so proud of them.

My heartfelt appreciation goes to Brian's beloved sister Pat, who, despite her own suffering, always managed to comfort me. I could not have coped without her unfailing emotional and physical support. She and Brian had endured much sadness in their lives and shared an extremely close and loving relationship because of it. Their father Vic passed away in his sleep after a period of breathlessness and an incident of fluid on his lungs which we now believe was due to mesothelioma. Their mother Dorrie passed away four months later of lung cancer. Tragically, seven short months spent in Wittenoom robbed Pat of her entire family. No one can imagine the immensity of such a loss.

I wish to express my gratitude to my parents and all family members who were there to listen, offer support and generously help us when anything physical needed to be done.

I want to especially thank my brother-in-law Dennis, who made it possible for Brian to have his last holiday in Exmouth and for caring for him in my absence.

FRIENDS

My sincere thanks goes to our good friend John Tate who understood Brian's need to continue fishing and gave his all to make it possible. He also worked tirelessly in our yard and looked after our home in our absence. We could not have managed without him.

I want to acknowledge and thank the Kailis' crew and all Brian's friends, old and new, who rallied to help his dream of a patio become a reality and generously donated their time and vehicles to help us relocate to Perth. And everyone, family and friends alike, who lovingly and generously contributed to our trip to Darwin.

AH CRAWFORD LODGE

Crawford Lodge, an establishment designed for, and available to, cancer sufferers and their families from the country, is a wonderful institution. Nothing has been spared to ease the burden of its inhabitants and the staff are wonderful; they are always there to listen and offer a genuine hug when needed. It is an oasis of peace amidst the chaos of sickness and death. For the short time I was there, it was sometimes the only light in a very dark tunnel.

My sincere appreciation and thanks to Dr Andrew Dean - Virtual Cancer Centre, Steve Carmody - Silver Chain Organisation and Jeannie Joughin - Mayne Pharmaceuticals, for their encouragement and generous financial assistance.

I wish to thank my proof reader for her help, and my father for his unwavering support of my writing. *The next one is for you, Dad.*

INTRODUCTION:

Apart from our own dying experience, we will never be closer to, or understand more, the process of dying than when we are the carer of a fellow human being with a terminal illness. Most often it is our loved one who we will be caring for, making the task even more overwhelming. To constantly bear witness to the ravages of the disease, knowing that you are powerless to stop its progression, is a huge burden.

Caring for the terminally ill brings many challenges. It will test you, humble you, reward you and painfully remind you of the fragility of life, the strong and mysterious flame that burns within us that can suddenly be blown out like a candle in the wind.

I write from my experience as a loving wife and carer to my late husband Brian, who passed away from pleural mesothelioma on 24 December 2001. This book portrays his journey through terminal illness, and the steps I took to ease his suffering and improve the quality of his life.

It also portrays, through my diary, the grief I suffered living with the expectation of his death and my growing strength as I came to realise that I was making a difference. In many ways my journey was one of discovery; it has shown me the true meaning of love and the strength of the human spirit.

Medications may change over time; the information I pass on to you regarding the management of pain and symptom control is timeless.

Regardless of the medication taken, good communication between your loved one, yourself, and the doctor is the key to a better quality of life. Together you can make a difference.

Not everyone will choose to do as I have done. Some may wish to and not be able to carry it through. Do not persecute yourself, or feel that you have failed if you are unable to care for your loved one at home. You can only do your best. Your understanding, and your efforts to ease their suffering, will improve the quality of their life and their death, even if they are hospitalised.

May God be with you all.

IN THE BEGINNING:

I was fourteen years old when my school friend introduced me to her cousin Brian. He seemed shy but after awhile he relaxed and we talked easily. He told me that he lived in Port Hedland and was enjoying a holiday in Perth; no mention was made concerning the length of his stay and I looked forward to seeing him again. I was disappointed to learn that, shortly after our meeting, he returned home. Six months passed before he came back to Perth and changed the course of my life.

I can still remember how excited I was when he rang to ask me out and the blue check shirt and grey trousers he wore when he came to meet my parents. I noticed his hair was shorter; it made his ears stick out, but his smile hadn't

Brian and Me - *courting days*

changed and I felt the same butterflies in my stomach as I had when we first met. My family, instantly at ease, invited him to join us in a game of Monopoly. I found it impossible to concentrate and spent my time sitting shyly beside him imagining what it would be like when he kissed me.

Later that evening, we drove to the local drive-in theatre, both suffering from first date nerves. It seemed to be taking a long time for the gates to open and it was with some amusement that we realised we were waiting at the exit gates.

I don't remember the movie but I will never forget his first kiss; from the moment our lips met I knew that we belonged together. We dated steadily for four years and were married when I was almost nineteen.

Our Wedding Day *1969*

Because we married young there were some rough times, many brought about by our eagerness to furnish our new home. We found it easy to obtain hire-purchase and took out several, placing strain on our dual incomes. When I became pregnant unexpectantly with my first child Michelle, Brian found it impossible to cover the house payments and bills on his wage and it became necessary to sell our house and furniture to clear the debts. Shortly after our second child, Clint, was born, we bought a caravan and headed for Useless Loop near Shark Bay.

Having spent my entire life in the city, I was unaccustomed to the extreme temperatures of the north; this, and the incessant bush flies, took some adjusting to, but it was the isolation that affected me most. I missed my family and friends and all of the things I had taken for granted. Living in a caravan with two small children was not easy, especially since Brian was a shift worker, but despite the hardships there was an upside. Away from the hustle and bustle of the city, people were more relaxed and genuinely friendly. In time I grew to love the free-and-easy lifestyle.

Brian spent most of his spare time fishing; I often went with him and came to enjoy it almost as much as he did. Mullet netting was one of our favorite pastimes. We also loved a good game of cards and spent many evenings with friends playing euchre.

After two years at the Loop, we decided to move to Jurian Bay where employment was available with Western Mining; this came with accommodation and I looked forward to living in a house again. Shortly before Brian was to commence, he met a cray fisherman at the local hotel and decided to become a deck hand. Fortunately we were able to find a house to rent.

Brian loved working on the boat but it was seasonal, and the wage not sufficient to support us for the rest of the year. Through a chance meeting with an old friend we learned that work was available at the mineral sands mine in Eneabba and decided to take a look at the town before making any decisions.

I could not believe my eyes when I first saw this little town nor imagine us living there, but full-time employment, plus a company house, was too good an opportunity to miss.

We were pleasantly surprised by the genuine friendship offered to us; Brian began work in production and soon after, I obtained casual work at the laboratory in town. Social life in Eneabba was a family affair and barbecues a way of life; they were a great way to unwind and many a good joke was told around the campfire. I became renowned for my contributions.

Country towns are wonderful for bringing up a family; Michelle and Clint revelled in the freedom, and around a year after our arrival I gave birth to our third child, Julie. Later, when she began school, I began working at the mine.

For seven years I worked in the Rehabilitation Department where I was a part of a team responsible for rehabilitating the mined areas. It was a challenging and often tedious occupation. We were always exposed to the elements and our seed-picking ventures often put us in danger of snake bite, but it was great fun and the camaraderie had no equal. My time in the Rehab. Dept was the most pleasurable and rewarding period of my working life.

The Rehab crew - *me third from the left on seed picking venture*

The coastal town of Leeman, twenty minutes drive from Eneabba, was a welcome respite from the heat and we travelled there often to go fishing. Occasionally we camped on the beach and our enjoyment of this resulted in the decision to erect a shack. Brian's sister, Pat, and her husband Noel joined with us, sharing the cost of its construction and upkeep. We were proud of our shack; it was more like a cottage than a humpy, with all the comforts of home, and an endless view of the ocean from our kitchen table.

For me the shack represented relaxation; I loved nothing more than to get stuck into a good book whilst being lulled by the sound of the waves crashing on the shore. Brian, on the other hand, rarely rested; for him the shack provided a perfect opportunity to do what he loved best. He spent most of his time on the water, happily providing us with ample fish and crays. He also loved to cook and we all anticipated and enjoyed the many tasty meals he concocted for us.

Our shack was a wonderful escape where, over the years, we spent many happy times with our family and friends. We were all saddened when the Shire of Carnamah declared that squatters were no longer permitted and we had to pull it down.

The Shack

Whilst Brian's passion was fishing, mine was music; I loved to sing and play the guitar and found ample opportunities when I joined the local repertory club. Over the years we performed a number of concerts and plays in Eneabba and the surrounding towns.

After years in production, Brian transferred to the stores and I left the Rehab. to take up the position of receptionist. Eighteen months later we decided to move to Perth. We had spent twenty years in Eneabba; it had been good to us, but it was time for a change.

We decided to try our hand at business and purchased a fish and chip shop in Mandurah; though highly successful, the long hours left little time to enjoy our new home and no time for our family and friends. After a while this got me down and I was relieved when we sold it.

We remained in Mandurah for a short time; however, Brian was eager to return to the North and when Clint moved to Exmouth, we followed. Brian had a special bond with Clint through their love of the ocean. Neither one of them could stay away from it for long.

Exmouth is predominantly a tourist town with little industry. Jobs are scarce, so we decided to start up our own business. After a lot of brainstorming we came up with the idea of retailing goods from Bali and made enquires about premises to lease. We were disappointed to learn that the one shop available to us was far smaller than we needed; furthermore it was situated in a narrow arcade, its windows overlooking a brick wall. We were concerned about the lack of passing trade; however, I was determined to go ahead. I had done my homework and was confident "The Bali Shop" would do well. I believed good advertising would attract both locals and tourists.

Anxious to have it up and running in time for the tourist season, I begun setting up contacts and importing clothing, shoes and artifacts directly from Bali. I then travelled to Exmouth to get it underway whilst Brian remained in Perth to settle the sale of our home. Aware that our income would fluctuate, Brian applied for work at Kailis', the local prawn factory, to supplement the leaner months.

The smallness of the shop created problems; there was a lot of stock and very little room in which to display it. Clint and his wife Dee were marvelous and spent hours helping me to erect the racks and mark the stock ready for sale.

On the night before opening we worked into the early hours, the grandchildren asleep on mattresses beside us. Our first day of trade surpassed all our expectations. We were so excited when I brought the first money bag home; I could hardly wait to tell Brian. As I had anticipated, The Bali Shop took off well. I found that being in business presented many challenges and I thrived on them.

Exmouth has a unique lifestyle and Brian revelled in it; he was an avid shell collector as well as a keen fisherman and had a vast knowledge and respect for shells and their habitat. He would walk for miles in pursuit of a specimen to add to his sizable collection.

We spent many happy hours with Clint, Dee and the children camping at the beach. Often Michelle, her fiancé Mark, and Julie would join us and it was wonderful for us all to be together. The men spent most of their time fishing and our faithful dog, Ben, loved to join in; how he managed to execute a series of lunges, given the depth of the water, remains a mystery, but despite his valiant efforts he never caught a fish. He loved to eat them raw and would station himself beside us at cleaning time eagerly awaiting any tidbits we sent his way.

Campsite - *Pebble Beach Exmouth 1998*

These were special times; I loved to relax, enjoy a few cold drinks with my loved ones and watch the children as they played in the sand. When circumstances made it necessary for Clint and his family to move to Perth, we missed them terribly.

As the business flourished we decided to move into larger premises on completion of a new shopping complex. Though overheads were higher, the new venue was more accessible to the public and we were confident that this would increase our trade. Michelle decided to rent the shop next to ours for her natural therapy and massage business and I looked forward to having her near.

In January 1999 we flew to Bali to purchase stock; this was a particularly arduous time as we travelled by foot to each of our suppliers, widely spread throughout Kuta. In expectation of a busy tourist season we placed large orders. Brian was a shrewd businessman and very good at bartering; there were not many who could pull the wool over his eyes.

From Bali we flew to Singapore, then boarded a Garuda flight bound for New Zealand where we planned to holiday with Michelle and Mark. We felt uneasy due to the heavy rain, thunder and lightening raging around us. As the plane ascended, our worst fears became reality. Smoke wafted into the cabin, alarms began to sound and several attendants carrying fire extinguishers made their way down the aisle.

I was terrified and prayed that the plane would turn back to Singapore; however, it continued to ascend with all aboard fearing for our lives. Mercifully, a short time later, the smoke cleared and without explanation, the crew began serving meals. Brian and I had no interest in our food but we certainly enjoyed the drinks that came with it. I remember Brian saying, "Just give me a rotten red", his nickname for red wine.

We had a wonderful holiday, and thanks to Michelle and Mark we saw many of New Zealand's attractions. On several occasions Brian was less energetic than usual and he had a cold that had not cleared despite several doses of medication. He shrugged it off thinking that he had a dose of the flu.

There was much to do upon our return; stock to be unpacked and readied for sale. I spent hours ironing badly creased clothing. We were tired; we had crammed a great deal into a few weeks. However, we were excited about our purchases and looked forward to the start of the tourist season.

Mark, Michelle, Me and Brian - *Exmouth*

Brian's Sister Pat and husband Noel

Clint, Dee, Kameron, Shannon and Kylie

Brian & Grandaughter Shannon

Brian and Grandson Kameron

Brian & Grandaughter Kylie

On the 22 March 1999, Category 5 Severe Tropical Cyclone Vance hit Exmouth. With winds reported at 300 kilometres an hour it was upgraded to a hurricane and documented as the most severe cyclone in Australian history. Exmouth was declared a national disaster. The devastation resembled a war zone. Just as the buildings had been swept up, dropped and shattered, so, too, had the hopes, plans and dreams of many.

Cyclone Vance - *Typical damage*

Having no control over our life was a new and disturbing experience. Our rental home was badly damaged, our furniture destroyed, and existence without power and water unbearable. We also had deep concerns regarding the future of our business; we had lost minimal stock to water damage but the cyclone had robbed us of tourist trade.

The local club, recognising the need for everyone to share experiences and support one another, put on an hour of free drinks each evening. I did not enjoy these occasions. Tired from lack of sleep and aggravated by the noise and false heartiness, I craved solitude, but even in this I found no peace.

It was amazing how quickly Exmouth began to recover, due to the spirit and determination of its residents and the generous physical and financial contributions from the army and voluntary organisations.

After much deliberation Brian and I decided to go ahead with our plans to relocate. I looked forward to the spaciousness of the new premises and the pleasure of looking out of my windows onto the street. There was a lot to be done and we were thankful for Michelle and Mark who worked tirelessly to help us. Despite the hard work, it was fun and we were excited and proud of our achievement.

I revelled in my new shop. It was a pleasure to work in and I was better able to cater to the needs of my customers. Unfortunately, I did not have Michelle's company for long; though well received, her business had limited clientele and the rent was high. Reluctantly she decided to close down and shortly after, she and Mark returned to Perth. I missed them; it was heartbreaking to be so far away from my children and grandchildren. I always felt I had been robbed of so much precious time.

My new Bali Shop - *September 1999*

The Bali Shop continued to flourish. It was a happy and rewarding time in which I was able to put the emotional scars of the cyclone behind me and regain my zest for living. I was not to know that the biggest trial of my life was soon to follow.

Content with our life in Exmouth, Brian and I decided to buy our own home. After several months we put an offer on a former Royal Australian Air Force house. It was built to withstand cyclones and had weathered Cyclone Vance well. Settlement was due on the 4 November, but as we had purchased it tenanted it was not available to us until May.

In December, Brian and I were walking home from a game of lawn bowls when I became aware of his shortness of breath. I was surprised and concerned when he told me that he had experienced this on several occasions. Believing this to be due to a chest infection, I made a doctor's appointment for him the next day. Chest X-rays revealed fluid on the lungs, over two litres of which was drained, giving Brian immediate relief, but it was a tense wait for the pathology results.

Through the Internet I had become aware of several conditions which may have been responsible for fluid on the lung; these included asbestos - related diseases. Brian had lived in Wittenoom as a child and I was afraid of his diagnosis. Not wanting to worry him unnecessarily, I did not mention my fears to him. I prayed that he had pleurisy or pneumonia but the pathology results revealed that there were cancer cells present.

TERMINAL DIAGONOSIS:

When Brian finally received his diagnosis, my worst nightmare became reality. He had pleural mesothelioma, a terminal cancer of the lung caused by the inhalation of asbestos dust. We were still reeling from the shock when, without preamble, the young doctor gave his prognosis. His exact words were, "Three to nine months, I reckon". That he could say this so unfeelingly amazed me. His total lack of compassion did not encourage even the small comfort of tears. I felt as if Brian and I had been shot and from that moment on we were waiting to drop.

Undoubtedly, we *were* mortally wounded. We suffered shock, disbelief, anger, helplessness and utter despair; in fact all the symptoms of grief one feels when a loved one has actually died. Once again we found ourselves with no control over our lives, but this time there was no light at the end of the tunnel. Our journey through terminal illness had begun.

I cannot remember the walk to the hospital car park where our three children were waiting. I do remember the five of us huddled in the cocoon of our car, holding each other, our tears now falling freely. The children and I, united in our love for Brian, held him, comforted him and determined that nothing was going to steal him from us. We found it inconceivable that his disease was the result of inhaling asbestos dust as a child and that it had lain dormant for forty-five years before becoming lethal.

We decided that if the medical profession could not save him, we would, and purchased antioxidant tablets, colloidal silver, and vegetable and mineral supplements to strengthen his immune system. We then consulted a naturopath who recommended we invest in a Rife machine. We had never heard of this; he explained that many people believed the electric frequencies transmitted through this machine had the ability to shrink tumours. I was sceptical and further discouraged by the exorbitant price tag of $4500, but it represented a ray of hope for Brian and I decided that, for this alone, it was worth the price.

Christmas was less than a week away but we had no heart for cheer and New Year's Eve 1999 was the saddest we had ever known. I found it impossible to fit back into the pattern of our days prior to Brian's diagnosis. I felt as if I had fallen off the planet, my distress intensified by the reaction of our friends and acquaintances who were shocked over our tragic circumstances, and not knowing what to say or how to act, avoided us.

At the local club, instead of the enthusiastic welcome we were accustomed to, we were greeted with silence, whispers or exaggerated attempts at joviality. It was as if we had lost our identity. They no longer saw us as Brian and Lorraine; we had become the objects of pity, a sad reminder to all of the fragility of life.

ACCEPTANCE

Throughout the course of our married life my deep love for Brian and my determination to resolve difficulties had seen us through many trials. I found it hard to believe that nothing could be done to save his life and begun surfing the Internet for information regarding mesothelioma, all the time praying for a miracle, hoping against hope to find a doctor who had successfully operated on or cured someone of it.

It was a sad realisation to discover that for Brian there were no miracles; however, I learned a lot and it helped me to accept that he was dying. This in no way made it easier to bear; we all must die but nothing can portray the anguish of knowing when. Living in expectation of Brian's death had a catastrophic effect on all of our lives.

Needing to express the depth of my love, I wrote Brian a letter telling him that although we had never won a lottery, we were rich in the wealth of love we shared and that I had always been happy knowing that he loved me. I thanked him for being a loving, hardworking and loyal husband, and for providing all the material things I had ever wanted. Added to this, I promised that he would not suffer unnecessary pain or die in hospital. With the letter I gave him the poem, "Loving You", which was the first of many I wrote throughout our journey to his death and beyond. I came to think of these poems as my "teardrops", so many of them fell during their creation.

Loving You

Every time I look at you I'm loving you
I send you tender kisses with my eyes
All my thoughts wrap my arms around you
To keep you safe and always by my side
I'd give the world if only I could save you
From the fate we know is just too hard to bear
For thirty-six years I've walked beside you
And I can't imagine life without you there
So down this frightening road we'll go together
Lean on me whenever you are tired
And if somewhere along the way we're parted
Wait for me I'll soon be by your side

Reluctant to spend one precious moment away from Brian I immediately put the business up for sale; this was not easy because I loved my shop and it hurt to let it go. Shortly after, due to increased breathlessness, Brian left his employ at Kailis'. It was a sad day for him as he enjoyed his work and the camaraderie of his fellow workmates.

Brian loved country and western music and had often expressed a desire to go to Tamworth; we decided to go while he was well enough to enjoy it and planned our trip around a Slim Dusty concert. He had long been an avid fan of Slim and looked forward to seeing him in person.

Tamworth is an amazing town; everywhere we turned there was a band playing or a singer strumming a guitar. We saw many young women performing and thought often of our daughter, Julie, who made the finals of Pop Stars and is eager to make it in the music world. She has a voice well-suited to country music and we determined that, upon our return, we would encourage her to participate in the next festival.

Brian and I - *Tamworth NSW 2000*

Though Brian appeared to be well, whenever he was out of my sight I worried that he would not return to me. At the train station he left to make enquiries and did not return within the expected time. Fearing that he had collapsed somewhere, I begun to panic; despite the huge crowd, I had never felt so alone. I asked a passer-by where the ticket office was then dragged the two heavy suitcases and his Rife machine all the way to it. The relief I felt at the sight of him knew no bounds.

ANTICIPATORY GRIEF

As the disease progressed Brian began to experience severe pain, partly due to the fluid which continued to accumulate, placing great strain on his organs.

I felt like I was drowning; his prognosis was always on my mind; I came to dread the beginning of each month, knowing that our time together was running out. Michelle was to be married in June but our anticipation was clouded by the knowledge that Brian might not be alive to enjoy it. I had no way of knowing how long he would survive and saw every symptom as an indication of his impending death. I began to feel tightness in my chest, often became short of breath, and groaned involuntarily. I needed my family and, after weeks of repressing my anxiety, I told Brian that I wanted to move to Perth. His reaction was explosive. He said, "You are wallowing in self pity!" His words wounded me deeply, causing my pent-up emotions to burst from me and I totally lost control. I threw every thing I could lay my hands on around the room and screamed until I could scream no longer. Finally, exhausted, I fell to the floor and sobbed. Brian came to me; he had not meant to hurt me. I understood and forgave him.

I wished there was someone I could talk to, but I had nowhere to turn. My children were trying to come to terms with their own grief and it upset them if I made any mention of their father's deterioration. At times I felt that I was the only one who believed he was dying.

I was determined to walk beside him on the journey to the end of his life and to keep the promises I had made, but I needed to know what he was experiencing and what I could do to alleviate his suffering. Once again I surfed the Internet, this time to find out about pain. I then made the first of many appointments with Brian's doctor where we discussed this and the drugs which were available to manage it.

He prescribed MS Contin, a slow-release morphine tablet which was to be taken as a means of stable control and explained that stronger doses would be required as Brian's disease progressed. He then asked how I was coping; I immediately burst into tears. He was very understanding and told me that the despair I felt was *anticipatory grief*, due to the expected death of Brian. He believed that I should not mask my grief with anti-depressant drugs and recommended that I see a counsellor on a regular basis. He also suggested that I keep a personal diary. His advice was sound; the diary I began on that day became my strongest coping tool. Since I could not share my fears with Brian, or unburden myself to our children, it became my closest ally. I wrote in it almost every day, pouring my heartache onto the pages.

I can't imagine how Brian copes with the knowledge that he is dying. I wake with such sadness and dread of the coming months that it is all I can do to keep going. It is hard not being able to unburden myself to him as I have always done; we are both trying to be strong for each other. It is so sad that when we need support and comfort we cannot turn to each other and voice our fears.

I miss his strength; he can no longer wrestle with me, hold me or lay beside me without feeling pain. We are all grieving even before he has died; the time left to share is always tinged with sadness. I am seriously considering sending our story to the publishers of major magazines. I want everyone to know what is happening to us and that someone is responsible for this tragedy ...

It is hard when people are always watching us to see how we are coping. I try to behave normally, but then I think, how can I be normal? Brian is dying. Sometimes when we are with friends, he laughs and I am happy for him. But if I laugh, I feel guilty. I have no right to laugh or to feel normal so I deliberately make myself sad by looking at Brian and reminding myself that I am losing him. Last night one of the ladies said to me. "You are such a strong woman". What makes her think that? I don't feel strong; I am trying to appear strong for Brian but inside I am breaking.

It amazes me that I can appear calm when I am far from calm. I am angry! I could lose the plot at any time. Knowing that Brian is dying is like sitting on a time bomb that could go off at any moment, and being powerless to stop it. Today Julie grabbed me and twirled me around the room; I was so stiff I felt as if I could snap in half. It made me realise how tightly I am holding myself together, but I dare not loosen my grip, if I do, I will not be able to cope.

The counsellor cried when I told her my story. She agrees that I should not take anti-depressants. I like her; I hope she can help me. Pat is leaving soon. I will miss her a lot; somehow she always manages to comfort me. I feel a little better after the huge cry I had on her shoulder this morning. I am so lucky to have her.

Brian now gets hot and sweaty at night and I fear what this new development means. He is in pain again; the fluid is coming back. I wish I could find a way to stop it. Is the machine doing anything to shrink his tumour?

I cannot bear the thought of him not being beside me as I grow older. I am afraid of what lies ahead: the pain, the suffering and the ache of losing him. He looks amazing considering what he is going through. I feel like I am falling apart. Tonight I cannot sleep. I am sitting here at 2.10 am and, despite taking a sleeping pill, I am not tired. There is a constant ache between my shoulder blades. I wish I could find someone to talk to. But who? I need to have a good cry. If I don't find some relief soon I will break down again.

I have put on a lot of weight, rarely wear make -up and my hair is a mess. I care but I don't care. I am depressed. Our life has changed so dramatically. How am I supposed to feel when giving Brian morphine has become routine? When his managing to go to the toilet is good news? When something coming after the month of September brings incredible sadness? And ever in my mind is the thought of him dying?

It is Mother's Day today. The kids rang and I rang my mum. Nothing means a great deal to me anymore. My world has become the confines of this house, and Brian and I within it. Mum and Dad call me often and Sandra, Jude and Di send e-mails. It's good to talk to them. After I have unburdened myself I always feel guilty to have caused them distress, but I know I will do it again when I need to and that they will understand.

I'm in such turmoil; I don't know how to feel, what to think or how to go on with this terrible strain. Brian's pain is not under control despite the increase in medication and when he is in pain, I am in pain. I'm so tired of trying to act as if everything is okay when nothing is okay. Brian is dying! I torture myself by imagining what it will be like when he no longer walks in the front door, comes down the passage to greet me, or calls me on the phone. What will I do when I can never reach him again? Never hear the sound of his voice, the sound of his footsteps or his breathing beside me? I often think it would be easier to die with him, but I could not do that to my children. I hate letting him out of my sight; I am afraid that he will die and I will not have the chance to say goodbye...

I continued to seek knowledge about mesothelioma and became aware of the symptoms Brian would experience as the disease progressed; this and my understanding of pain and its management was to have a huge impact on the quality of his life - and mine. As my efforts continued to ease his suffering, I realised that although I could not save him from dying, I *could* help him to live. This removed my feelings of helplessness and gave me strength.

UNDERSTANDING PAIN:

Pain is a word, and like many in the English language, it has more than one meaning. To begin with, there is *emotional pain* and there is *physical pain*. It is important to recognise and treat both.

Dealing with terminal illness is a heartbreaking experience which dramatically affects the emotions of the patient *and* their loved ones. This often results in depression which can cause a variety of symptoms: sleeplessness, nausea, anxiety, shortness of breath, change of bowel habits, lack of appetite, excessive appetite, isolation, anger and thoughts of suicide.

Depression is a normal reaction to stress and feelings of helplessness but you must not let it overwhelm you. Don't be afraid to talk to your doctor, or to seek counselling. Speaking to a counsellor on a regular basis will ease many of the pent-up emotions you are experiencing. It is also helpful to keep a personal diary. In it record everything you are feeling, even your darkest, deepest thoughts and fears. It will not judge you.

There are medications available to treat depression; however it is better that you do not rely upon them. A good cry is the simplest and most effective way to relieve tension; it is healing and leaves only the stain of tears upon your cheeks.

Physical pain can present itself in many ways; it may be stabbing, dull aching, throbbing, tingling, burning or even cramp-like. It can also have varying intensities. Not all pain will respond to the same medication. For instance, a tingling pain is often caused by nerve damage. Interestingly, this often responds to drugs which are primarily used for depression.

PAIN MANAGEMENT:

Whilst the majority of cancer patients do experience chronic pain, only a small percentage of them have *adequate* pain relief. This is often due to the common belief that large doses of medication, such as morphine and methadone (used for pain control in cancer sufferers), will sedate them and prevent them from functioning normally. Sadly, many people suffer unnecessarily due to this misconception.

Unrelieved pain causes short concentration span, sleep disturbance, anxiety, depression, anger, isolation, and thoughts of suicide. Taking morphine or methadone for pain associated with disease must not be compared with drug addiction. Correctly prescribed, it does not result in a "high", nor does it result in sedation. Chronic pain effectively "uses up" medication.

The object of pain management is to *always be in front of the pain.* Good communication with your loved one is imperative; so too is their honesty in relating to you, the nature and intensity of their pain. Encourage them not to brave it out by letting it reach debilitating levels before asking for relief. This results in a situation where they are chasing the pain instead of being in front of it. *Untreated chronic and debilitating pain kills. It kills the will to live.*

Despite the large doses of medication Brian took regularly, he remained active and alert, drove his car for eighteen months after diagnosis and did not become bed bound until three days prior to his death.

USING A PAIN SCALE:

A pain scale, using degrees of 0 to 10, is a means by which pain intensity can be noted and acted upon. The scale is an invaluable tool; it will allow your loved one to communicate the degree of their pain to you knowing that you will understand, and more importantly, that you can do something about it.

KEEPING A JOURNAL:

Another tool necessary to attain good pain management is a journal; an ordinary exercise book will do. Set out a page for each day. Make a list of all the medications to be taken and against each one record the dosage and the times they are to be administered. Place a tick against them as they are given. Also make note of any pain that is experienced; be careful to describe its *type* and *intensity* using the pain scale. Any changes in wellbeing, no matter how small, should be recorded.

Remember to take your journal with you on every visit to the doctor. He will appreciate your input; it will help him to understand how your loved one is coping and make it possible for him to adjust medication as necessary.

BREAKTHROUGH PAIN:

Breakthrough pain is a term used to describe pain that *comes through* despite regular medication. As a general rule, if pain is still severe twenty minutes after medication is given, stronger doses are necessary. Periods of breakthrough must be recorded in your journal and related to the doctor on your next visit. He may prescribe hydromorphone for such incidences; it is fast acting and very effective.

Hydromorphone worked well for Brian. We used it as necessary until, upon our next visit, his stable medication was adjusted to meet the new level of pain he was experiencing.

SYMPTOM CONTROL:

Symptoms will vary with each person and can be a result of medication, disease progression, or both.

CONSTIPATION:

One of the most common and debilitating side effects of strong pain medication is constipation. Many patients believe that this must be endured. This is incorrect. Bowel management can be achieved so that constipation is no longer suffered, regardless of the amount of pain medication taken.

In order to achieve this it is important that you are aware of the first sign of difficulty so that you can do something about it *before* it gets to the debilitating stage. Cereals, Metamucil, and the like cannot relieve the severity of this condition; you will need to work with your doctor to find a solution.

Brian suffered severe constipation due to morphine. His doctor prescribed senokot and bisacodyl. They did not relieve his condition and he became distressed. Had this symptom continued, the uncomfortable and embarrassing solution would have been manual extraction.

Once again I turned to the Internet and it was there that I learned about parachoc. This is a paraffin-oil-based preparation in the flavors of chocolate or vanilla and can be purchased at the chemist without prescription. The introduction of this, added to the senokot and bisacodyl, controlled Brian's bowels perfectly.

At times, especially after chemotherapy, he did not require the same amount of bowel medication and, through our good communication, we adjusted it. He never experienced constipation again, a remarkable achievement considering the large amount of morphine he was on.

It is important that the doctor is aware of all the medications your loved one is taking. If you decide to give the parachoc, introduce it slowly. Brian needed only 10 mls each morning; it is not recommended to be taken at night.

SWOLLEN LEGS AND FEET:

Another common symptom is painfully swollen legs and feet. We found that this can be controlled by the use of diuretics.

Any symptoms your loved one experiences should be noted in your journal and discussed with your doctor. He will then be able to prescribe medication to bring them under control.

Due to the nature of Brian's disease, and the symptoms it presented, it was a never-ending battle to ease his suffering. Keeping him out of pain became the reason for my existence, but despite my efforts, there were many times when his pain broke through and this upset me terribly. I have no doubt, however, that my continual quest to bring his pain and symptoms into control eased his suffering and improved the quality of his life.

Well, it is another day and Brian is sitting in front of his Rife machine. I am so grateful for it. I can't imagine what he would be like if he had only the vitamin pills to pin his hopes on ... I feel like a trapped animal. The guard I have built around my heart is so fragile. Each time a new symptom shows up, or if he is in pain and I cannot stop it, I suffer. What can I do to get me through this? Is there anyone out there who can help me? I think not. I am incredibly lonely; I have lost so much of Brian already. I wish with all my heart that I could save him. I feel as if my pot is empty and I have not the emotional energy to put anything back into it ...

Sorrow

My life has become a burden of sorrow

Living each day - no plan for tomorrow

Seeing my loved one die a little each day

The doctor can't save him

He said - No way

For forty-five years in his lungs it waited

Before sending its cancerous spread

Three to nine months - the doctor said

And your husband will be dead

Today I went to the doctor; she told me that my aching arms were probably a result of massaging Brian all the time and added that they could also be aching due to anxiety. "You look unhappy," she said, "You look stressed." Big observation! I am unhappy, I am stressed. Who wouldn't be? I'm bored with being at home all day. Nothing to do but go fishing or watch television. I want to go to Perth; we could spend more time with the kids. I miss work; never thought I would but there it is. I miss the challenge and the sense of achievement in a job well done. I understand how Brian must miss Kailis'; the absolute nothingness of our day-to-day existence is soul destroying.

I am so consumed with Brian's welfare and the precious time we have left together that I have no time or energy for anything else; his impending death is forever on my mind. I am lost in the enormity of it all. It has occurred to me that if I don't change my mental attitude, I will become ill. I do want to live; I have a great deal to live for through my children and grandchildren. I am still young and I will survive this if I allow myself to. I must start looking after myself, as well as Brian, if I am to remain healthy. Who am I to wish life away when Brian is trying so hard to hang on to it?

MY DAILY AFFIRMATIONS WILL BE:

I will do my best to ease the burden for Brian
I will do my best to remain positive for the both of us
I will make each day as peaceful and as happy as I can
I will count my blessings for each day we share together
I will take care of my body and my mind and believe that
I have plenty of reasons for living
I will imagine my immune system working hard to keep me healthy
I will survive and carry on
I will embrace life and live it to the fullest for the remainder
of my days

I was just reading through yesterday's notes. The words are all very well, but can I do it? I have some days where I'm okay and others where I am devastated. I am devastated! It is all so unfair - why is this happening to us? I want it all to go away. I want a future with Brian. I love him so much.

Brian had the fluid off again today, I knew as soon as he walked in the door that it had not gone well. He looked sick, old and frightened; it was like looking through a window into the future. He has more cramping stiffness in his side, and under his left rib, and the sweats are continuing. Though the strength of his slow-release morphine tablets has been increased, he still wakes in pain during the night and he is starting to show the strain. I am going to get on the Internet again to find out if anything else can be done ... It will soon be his birthday. I want to do something special for him and for our anniversary but Exmouth is so isolated. What can I arrange to bring him joy? If only we had twenty more years together. I wish I could reach into his body and draw the cancer from him or give one of my lungs to save him...

Various medications were prescribed to control the progressive symptoms of Brian's disease but it was not until the introduction of liquid morphine that we begun to experience more efficient control. I continued to use the pain scale and communication with him to determine the nature and intensity of his pain and found we achieved better results if I gave him smaller doses of the liquid morphine at two-hourly intervals, rather than the larger dose four-hourly.

I have read a lot about caring for a cancer patient and it amazes me that I am already doing all the things they recommend. I am proud of what I have achieved on my own. It means a lot to Brian that I am able to help him. Without the things I have learned on the Internet, I would not be able to work with the doctor and the chemist to ease his pain. I must find out who I can ring if something happens at night; I need to know that someone will be there for me ...

Brian had remarkable willpower and immeasurable courage. He strove to get on with his life despite his illness and I strove to make this possible for him. For a short time we were able to continue playing lawn bowls and have a few drinks at the bar before the game. My bag always held two doses of medication, allowing for some freedom from the house. I would unobtrusively hand this to Brian when due and he would swallow it, grimace and then down another beer. Our friends had begun to relax in our company and we enjoyed these occasions immensely.

Brian is much better today. He is not as tired and his colour is good. He still looks beautiful to me and I find myself thinking over and over that this cannot be happening. I wish I could afford the luxury of hope. But the signs are all there for me to see. I cannot be fooled by him having a good day; I know it is the medicine that makes him feel better. The swelling on his back has grown; I think it is the tumour. He is always asking me to rub it for him; it eases the pain for a little while. Why is his stomach so distended? Is the fluid building up there as well?

We had a nice day for Brian's birthday. His medication is working well. It is good to see him moving more freely and able to sleep through the night. On the doctor's advice he is also taking panadol four times a day. Apparently this aids the morphine into his system. I capture a million pictures, words and hugs to keep in my heart ... The other day a good friend asked me how I was. I found it hard to answer her truthfully. I don't know how I am. I think that I am coping but when Brian cannot get his breath, I panic, fearing that he is having a heart attack. My reaction worries me. I need to be strong for him ...

June arrived, Brian mercifully still with us, and we allowed ourselves to feel excited about Michelle's wedding. Shortly before we flew to Perth, he had the fluid drained so that he would not be breathless on the day.

The wedding was all we hoped it would be; Michelle looked beautiful and Brian's face was beaming as he proudly walked her down the aisle. Seeing him resplendent in his suit made me think of our own wedding day and reminded me of how true and abiding our marriage was. "In sickness and in health, until death us do part." The words hung in the air and landed in my heart.

Thankfully Brian's pain remained in control and he was able to enjoy this special day. As a surprise, Michelle had arranged for a piper; he loved to hear them and it was wonderful to see his pleasure. Julie, our little song bird, sung a special song for her sister. I was so proud of my children and of my husband as he mingled with the guests and later gave a speech full of his customary humour.

Brian giving his speech

Michelle's Wedding Day - *June 2000*

Brian proudly walks Michelle down the aisle

Michelle, Brian, Mark and Me

Today Brian had the fluid off again and came home ill. I made him a sweet cup of tea and rubbed his back. He told me that coming home to me always makes him feel better. When he puts his arms around me I feel the solidness of him, the warmth of him, the feel of his skin and hair next to mine, and I want to cry. But I try hard not to when we are together. I must remain strong for him. I don't want him to think that he must face the fear of death on his own ...

Something terrible happened today. We were at the Bay of Rest when a huge school of mullet passed us. In the excitement of herding them into the net, Brian over-exerted himself and the air in his mouth would not go down his throat and into his lungs. It was a terrifying experience for him, and for Clint and me; we did not know what to do. Thank goodness, Brian forced himself to relax and eventually his breathing returned. It shook us up for a long time; we all thought he was going to die. We now fear that this will happen again. The doctor has prescribed ventolin; it may ease his anxiety, but it is the fluid in his lungs causing his breathlessness and no matter how often it is drained, it continues to come back ... I am finding it hard to sleep. I am afraid that he is going to stop breathing.

I have read that anticipatory grief prepares the partner for the eventual death of their loved ones. I don't believe it. I think that it doubles the burden; I am grieving now, even while he is alive, and I will continue to grieve when he has died. The knowledge of his impending death is with me every waking hour and it is terrible... I am not excited about moving into our new house. What is the point? We will have to leave it before long.

It seems no matter how weak his body becomes, Brian's mind is stronger than ever. I can't stop looking at him and thinking, you are dying, you are dying. I have to do this to make myself believe I am losing him. I feel like I am on another planet, one filled with hopelessness and pain. Brian is dying but I still have the ability to hold him; kiss him, talk to him, laugh and cry with him. What will I do when these treasures are lost to me? I sometimes wish I was religious; I may then have found some solace, some peace and hope for a life thereafter. I can at least hope that the spirit does not die and that someday we may find each other again in another existence. Such a small thing to hold on to, but I have to grab for something, else I will be lost. I am glad now, that we decided to move into the house; it keeps me busy. Brian's friends have been marvelous and his dream of a patio will soon become reality. The garden is starting to look good too but there will be no joy in any of it after he has gone.

I can feel my control weakening as each new stage comes upon us. I desperately need to talk to someone - anyone - about what is happening to Brian and to me or I will surely go mad with the endless thoughts in my head. I can't believe that soon, too soon, I will lose him. Everywhere I look there is us, so many memories and things we have collected. I can't imagine life without him. How will I sort it all out? Where will I go? What will I do? We are trapped in this nightmare. No one can help us. There is no cure, no hope, and no future for us, only the black hole waiting.

The anguish of watching Brian become weaker makes it impossible to feel any sense of normality. I want him to hug me and hold me for as long as his arms can. I need to feel the essence of him. He has slept through most of the day and has hardly eaten because he has trouble swallowing. Sometimes when he sleeps he groans and looks so ill I fear that I am about to lose him, but then he wakes and talks to me and he looks and sounds so normal, so Brian that I think, no, he is not going to die, he is just tired. But in my heart I know, I know - and I can't stand the pain...

I went to the counsellor yesterday and spent over two hours talking to her. I hold nothing back and I am beginning to believe this helps me. I wish I could see her more than once a week She has told me not to let painful thoughts of the future take the enjoyment from our life together today. I can see the wisdom in this, but I worry how Brian will cope with each new stage of his disease. As long as I can control his pain, I think I will be able to hold up.

We have travelled even further on this reluctant journey. Brian's breathing has changed and increasingly he cannot swallow. I have known this will happen and tried to steel myself for it but it does not ease the sadness that this new stage brings upon us. He cried today; this is another step along the way. He is beginning to accept that he is dying. As terrible as it is to see him cry, I welcome it as I know that he badly needs to let it out. I told him he is allowed to cry and that he could talk to me about anything.

I have been dreaming a lot. In the early hours of this morning I dreamt that Brian was running full pelt towards me and I called to him not to. He kept running and fell, tumbling head over heels, but somehow managed to get up. The smile on his face was beautiful. I said something like, "You silly boy", and the next thing I woke up crying.

Well, September has come and gone and my darling is still with us. We have finished the patio at last; there has been such a crowd here helping us, and I am grateful, but it will be good to have a bit of quiet time. Nothing is normal. I miss our life, I miss Brian. I miss the yearning in his kiss and his want of me. I will never know these things again …

Michelle arrived today. It is good to have her with us… I have noticed that Brian perks up whenever someone comes to stay and is despondent when they leave. I, too, am affected by their absence; without the feeling of life they bring into our home I am lost. The kids are trying hard to be strong. My heart aches for them; they need special time with their father. I wish we lived in Perth. It would be so much better for us all.

I am in awe of Brian's courage. We talk now of the prognosis and I cry often - but only little cries in his presence. I still have feelings of wanting to die with him and told him so. He said, "The children will need you." This is true, but they have their lives ahead of them. I feel as if I am losing mine. In some ways I am because part of me will die when Brian dies. I still can't quite believe it. I am not ready to accept it now and no matter how many weeks pass, I will not be ready to accept it. I say to myself, yes, it is going to happen, but not now. Not three months from now. Not six months from now. I am not ready to lose him. I will never be ready to lose him.

Most times I hate leaving the house; it is our haven and we nurture each other here. Our world is no longer normal and within these walls it does not have to be. When I go amongst people I get extremely agitated and after a while I need to come back home. I get angry when I see old men because Brian will never be one. I am the most vulnerable when we are in each other's arms. I feel such love for him and wonder how much longer I will have his dear sweet body to hold. He came up behind me yesterday, put his arms around me, and nuzzled my neck. It is so beautiful when he does that. People tell me to live for today and not to worry about the future. How can I? How can I put the thought of losing Brian from my mind? I have read that you cannot live with the thought of death every day; I know this is true, because it is slowly but surely destroying me. My mind is always in turmoil. I wake with the same tiredness and hopelessness I go to bed with. My dreams are plagued with the same despair as all of my waking hours. I barely recognise myself in the mirror; my eyes are dull and lifeless on my face. A stranger looks back at me. I can see her pain ...

Today Brian went fishing. It was a beautiful sunny day with no wind and I was happy to see him go, knowing that he would enjoy himself. I had a good day too, potting plants and fussing around the house. For a little while I didn't think of pain and fear and death. I wish we could have at least one whole day where we could be free of these thoughts... Expectation of his death is wearing me down. I grow increasingly attached to the house; on some occasions I think I will be okay here after he dies and on others I think I will have to go away. There will be no place on earth where I can escape from the pain of losing him. I used to think that I would want to shut myself away when he dies but I know now that I will need people. I wish I had a friend. Who will be here for me when this is over?

Sometimes Brian and I get so wrapped up in what we are doing we feel quite high on the excitement of it. These times are so precious because, for a short time, we are able to feel normal. There are so many things going through my mind, so many things I need to know, but I do not know who to ask. I hate that we can no longer plan anything together; there's a great black void looming over us. I worry about our kids. They are suffering too, but I cannot help them. I am not as strong as I thought I was. I feel fragile. Yesterday, I told everyone I met that my husband was dying...

The fluid returns so quickly; Brian has just had his fifteenth aspiration. The doctor has told him to consider a pluerodesis. If this is successful it will ease his pain ... There are days when he feels well and I think I may have him for a while longer and then there are days where I think he is going to die. I cannot get away from this nightmare! What am I supposed to do? What am I

supposed to think? I am afraid of seeing him die, coping with the funeral and coming back here alone. The house will not be enough for me to live for ...

Brian continuous to refer to the future by saying, "If something should happen to me". I have come to realise that he alternates between acceptance and denial of his prognosis. It is hard to repress my feelings.

Yesterday I broke down and told him that I wanted to go to Perth because I was frightened of him dying in Exmouth and being alone to cope with it. We both cried. For a short time we were incredibly close, but then he drew away from me to control himself. I felt abandoned and continued to cry uncontrollably. I don't think I have ever sobbed so deeply or for so long in his presence.

I was terrified that my disclosure would ruin his enjoyment of the patio and his garden, and I could not bear that, but today he was out there as usual. Tonight he said that we would see how he was in a few months; if he was no longer able do the things he loves, then we might as well move to Perth. I wish we could move now. There is more to life than fishing. What about his children, grandchildren and sister? They need to spend more time with him before he dies. And I need to have their support while he is dying!

Tonight I drank a couple of Bacardi's; they must have gone to my head, as when I went down the street I was, just for a fleeting second, worry free. It felt amazing, foreign to me, and made me realise how much I would love the feeling of being happy again. How will I go on without Brian when there are so many things to remind me of him, of us? I don't want to spend the rest of my life alone. Will I ever be able to love someone else? Will I want to?...

Brian endured another seven aspirations, each of around four litres, before he decided to have the pleurodesis which involves the draining of fluid from the pleura and the placement of talc within it. In order to be successful, almost complete absence of fluid is necessary. Sadly, despite constant drainage, Brian's fluid continued to build up making it impossible to put the talc in place.

With pleurodesis no longer an option he faced a difficult decision - continue with the aspirations, or have a drainage tube put into his chest. The thought of a tube permanently protruding from his body worried him; however, the aspirations were painful and had become necessary on a weekly basis. He decided to have the tube put in place. Due to threat of infection, the entry site would have to be bandaged at all times and the dressing changed regularly.

Yesterday was the worst day since coming to Perth. A doctor came into Brian's room and immediately began to describe the tumour size and growth, its position in and around his organs, and his opinion of the time Brian had left to live. All this information, with no apparent reason or compassion, cut us to the core. I could not help but wonder why he delivered his news in such a brutal manner; all we needed to know was that the pleurodesis was not possible. We already knew that Brian was dying ...

Following the placement of the drainage tube, Brian's discomfort eased considerably; absence of fluid build-up in his lungs improved his breathing and he was once more capable of doing some of the things he loved. The visibility of the drainage bag and its contents, however, upset him, so I designed and made a cover for it. With clever use of tape and Velcro he was able to wear it close to his body where it was not conspicuous.

Jules will be up on Monday. I can't wait to see her. It will be hard for her to see how sick her father is ... Why is life so cruel? I need him to make love to me. I miss his nearness, the feel of his skin on mine, the deep loving kisses. I am lonely though he is with me still ...

It is hard to cope with my acceptance of his prognosis, whilst simultaneously recognising and supporting his need to live in hope of recovery. I encourage his hope but, at the same time, I am struggling to come to terms with my hopelessness. Sometimes I think, I will be strong, I will get on with my life, and then I think, I don't want to get on with my life. I want Brian. I want what I cannot have.

It is one night away from my fiftieth birthday but I cannot feel any joy or anticipation. The only thing I am grateful for is Brian being here to share it. I hate watching him get worse. I can't imagine what it will be like to see him die or to see him in a coffin. How do others do it? I don't know how long I will be able to cope with this grief. I have lost my own personality, confidence and drive. Will I ever recover from the ravages of this time? ...

For my birthday, Brian gave me a tiny golden heart and organised a small party. We both looked forward to seeing our friends and showing off our new house, but my party was not a happy one. Brian was too ill to participate, and I spent most of the night in tears.

In an attempt to defy his illness, Brian often pushed himself to the limit, resulting in pain for him and distress for me. I began watching him to make sure he didn't hurt himself. My constant pleading for him to take it easy, sit back in his chair, put his swollen feet up, irritated him, and on occasion, he would snap at me. His comments hurt, and angered me. They were undeserved, but I repressed my anger along with my sadness, loneliness, and fear because he was dying. There were several occasions, however, when I lost control; only at these times did I allow myself to sink into the true depths of my despair. I knew he never wished to hurt me; he was just trying to live. I came to understand that I had to allow him to do whatever he felt capable of doing. Sometimes his resulting pain took several hours to bring under control.

THE BAY OF REST

Despite his illness, there were times when Brian felt well and these were spent in the pursuit of his hobby, his passion, his true enjoyment of life, *fishing*. Most of the time I went with him, more to make sure he was okay than through my love of fishing. He was no longer able to lift the heavy motor onto the boat or pull the boat on and off the trailer, so our good friend John always came with us. Together, he and I would struggle to lift, pull and carry anything that was required. I don't know what we would have done without him.

Brian's favorite fishing spot was at the Bay of Rest; I used to affectionately call it the Bay of Unrest, as we did anything *but* rest there.

It was a long hot dusty drive to the Bay and the track was extremely bumpy. We would travel with Brian's fluid retaining bag on the seat between us, my hand pressed firmly over the tube entry site on his body to support it and ease the discomfort and pain caused by the jolting. My arm would ache and go numb but I never removed it until we reached our destination. Once Brian was so eager to get out of the car and into the boat, he forgot about the bag and the tube, and it caught on the gear stick. Thank goodness I was there to free it for him.

No matter how many times we went to the Bay, the routine never varied. The net was set, John and I collected the mullet, and Brian disappeared into the mangroves in pursuit of the elusive mangrove crabs. With his trusty hook in hand he never failed to pull them from their hiding places. Whenever he was out of sight, my anxiety escalated; I feared that he might collapse and die.

Brian with throw net - *Bay of Rest Exmouth*

Many times I sent John to find him but, thankfully, my fears were unfounded.

Sometimes, when the net failed to provide enough bait, Brian would use his throw net; he learnt the art as a child in Port Hedland and was very good at it. He could see the schools of fish in the water and, with the net held high on his shoulder, he would stalk them. When the time was right, he cast it in a perfect arc over the fish. As the net hit the water, the weights caused it to sink, trapping them within its pockets.

Next, it was time to get into the serious business of catching the mangrove jack. These are exciting fish to catch and have a habit of jumping up for the bait, especially if it has caught on the mangrove's roots above

Brian and Clint - *with Mangrove crabs Exmouth*

the water. Brian always sat at the back and steered the boat. John sat in the middle and I, cross-legged, on the bow. John had the chore of untangling my line when I heaved my catch into the boat.

There are special spots in the creek where the jacks are lively; we would cast the anchors, bait our hooks and there we would sit for the next four or five hours. My poor backside became numb, but when we were all pulling in the fish, I didn't feel it. I always had a supply of Brian's medicine on hand so that I could keep him out of pain no matter how long we spent on the water. I constantly marvelled at his ability to keep pulling in fish despite his lack of strength. I believe his love of fishing transcended any pain, weakness or discomfort he experienced.

We rose early to go to the Bay, so it was a long and tiring day by the time we drove home, cleaned the fish, and packed them away. Brian, however, would often want to return the next day, such was his love of it. I would try valiantly to talk him out of it - needing a day at least for my backside and aching back to recover but if he insisted, out we went again; both John and I found it impossible to deny him the pleasure. He was never more alive than when he was fishing. For him, at these times, there was no thought of sickness and death. For me, watching him, loving him, the thought of death was always on my mind.

Good Catch

Brian and John - *at the cleaning station*

Yesterday when I drove to the beach, I turned up the radio and sung along to the music. It felt good to focus on something else for a change. But it was not until I dived into the water that I realised how long it had been since I had truly felt alive. Every time I manage to free my mind of pain, someone asks me how Brian is, and it all comes crashing in. What do they want to hear? What can they possibly do or say that will make any difference? I feel like answering, how do you think he is? He is dying. He feels like shit. He is in pain and frightened of what is happening to him. Stop asking me and just leave me alone. I am sick and tired of acting as if my whole world is not coming to an end.

October has arrived and Brian is still with us; his health has continued to deteriorate and now when he sleeps I find myself checking to see if he is breathing. He is often irritated and does not want people around. Sometimes he cries and I long to comfort him, but he shuts himself away ...

Lonely

I miss our life

I feel like a mother - no longer a wife

I have no strong arms to hold me

No kisses to stir me

No loving to thrill me

No hope to sustain me

I feel alone in the darkest time of my life

Where will I find the strength to carry on

And to witness what I fear the most

Who will support me

I am so afraid

I am so lonely

Deep within the woman of me

I am already alone

The fluid has dried up due to the progression of the disease. Brian no longer needs the tube and it is such a relief for him not to carry the bag. He is breathing a lot easier now and can walk longer distances and climb steps without fear. The doctor has told us that he is breathing on one lung. I wish it was possible to remove the diseased one and save him, but the cancer is in the pleura surrounding both and it will affect the good one before long…

Last night I dreamed Brian choked on some food, fell backwards, and died right in front of me. I have not been able to put this from my mind. I feel isolated in my grief but I do not really want anyone's company …

I have begun to hate Exmouth. I wish we could go to Perth; I want to be close to my children, I want to do something - anything that is different from the day-to-day predictability of this godforsaken place.

Well, here it is, Christmas again. Clint, Dee and the kids are with us; the girls and Mark arrive tomorrow. It will be wonderful to be together but difficult with all of us in the house at one time … I can't believe the changes that have been forced upon us. The whole situation is terrible; we don't know what to expect. We know Brian is dying but how? When? Will he have a heart attack? Will I go in one morning to find him dead in bed? Will he go to the shop one day and not come back?

Christmas Day was nice; we had a present-opening ceremony and Clint recorded it on video. What memories there will be for us in the future. Julie gave Brian a compact disc with a song she had written and recorded especially for him, called "A Moment in Time", the words, so hauntingly beautiful, made it hard not to cry...

Brian was fairly good for most of the day and managed to eat lunch, a blessing as he had looked forward to it so much. The next-door neighbours came over with some friends and ended up staying for ages but it was good and did create a party atmosphere. Everything we did made me think about what the next Christmas will be like.

It is getting harder; I am giving him all the strength and nourishing that is in me but there is nothing coming back in, I feel empty. I can never get close enough to him. I wrap myself around his back and massage his sore spots but I am aching for him to be wrapped around me, massaging me, loving me ...

Who am I Now

Who am I now - this woman called Lorraine

Just a shadow of her former self

Such sadness - where shall I hide

I cannot put this grief aside

Where is my laughter - my love of life

I am now my dying husband's wife

I - like a mother - tend his every need

His body has become my mind

I have left myself - Lorraine - behind

Today we went to the beach; Brian hardly had the energy to throw the ball for Ben. I could see how much this upset him. It has been a year since diagnosis. What a year it has been. The kids say he looks good and I suppose he does, considering, but they don't see what I see...

The New Year has arrived and everyone has left for home. It has been good but I need some peace and quiet and a chance to be alone with Brian. The distance between us and the family has created an all-or-nothing situation which makes it hard for everyone. It would be far better if we lived in Perth, we could see each other often but still retain our own homes and routines.

I wonder how Brian feels about me now. He no longer desires me and probably doesn't register my looks very often. It saddens me to think that he may not miss making love to me. Is this why I let myself go? Am I trying to suppress my need by becoming fat and unattractive?

There are times when I want to run screaming into the street and others where I want to crawl into a little ball and hide in the closet. Of course, no matter where I run or hide, my head and all its thoughts will come with me. There would be no escape...

Today was not a good day ... Brian woke in severe pain and told me that it felt like the weight of a truck was resting on his chest. He has spent most of the day in bed or asleep in his chair. It is one thing knowing that he is dying and another having to witness it; I am constantly wondering when and how it will happen. We have increased his medication but it is not strong enough. I don't think it is capable of controlling the crushing pain he experiences from the tumour pressing against his organs. I can almost picture the bloody thing destroying him. He can't do much of anything any more. I don't know how he manages to get up in the morning and act as if there is a reason to carry on.

I have become the watcher - always watching whatever Brian does with a terrible fear that he may suddenly die ... Yesterday we went fishing and I worried all day about him running out of breath and having a heart attack. I try to do all the lifting and carrying so that he does not have to, but I know that this upsets him. Sometimes I think, let him do what he loves; if the effort takes him, at least he was happy. Then I think, no, don't let him do that, I am not ready to lose him. Is this selfish of me? Probably, but I will never be ready to lose him ...

It is hard to endure with this heavy burden. I am putting bricks into a wall which surround my emotions; I place a brick almost every day. The wall is my acceptance of Brian's impending death and the knowledge that I will soon be on my own. It is my reality. There is no hope of a cure. I must keep building the wall. It is the only thing that will hold me up when the time comes ...

Pain

Pain on black wings glides in to sit upon your shoulder

Digs its talons into your spine

shatters our peace - yours and mine

Robs me of your smile - robs us of days worthwhile

Reminds us of despair waiting for us everywhere

Pain - sister of the cancer's spread

within the breathing core of you

So close to your heart - beating for the both of us

Your breath - my world

Your life and mine intricately combined to be almost as one

I feel like I too am dying

We are dying

The partnership of us is dying

Too soon it will be - I instead of we - me instead of us

And widow instead of wife

In time, as my knowledge grew, I came to realise that many of Brian's symptoms were side effects of his medication, and those which arose due to the progression of his disease did not necessarily indicate that he faced imminent death. My understanding of the expected stages and symptoms of mesothelioma allowed for me to be one step ahead of its progression. In this way I was able to deal with the changes emotionally before they happened and be strong for Brian when he needed me most. It also gave me the opportunity to have medication and, later, physical aids on hand before he needed them; this alleviated much of the fear, pain and discomfort he would otherwise have suffered.

Brian and I have become closer than we could ever have imagined. My love for him is beyond measure. We are never far from each other's side and hold hands like we did in the old days ... We have made some big decisions; they have not been easy but there is a measure of peace in knowing that we have made them together. Clint arrives tomorrow; it will be good to see him.

I am struggling to come to grips with the reality of losing Brian and having to witness his suffering as he becomes more aware of his mortality. He makes plans for our house and it makes me want to stay here after he has gone so that I can do the things he envisioned but I want to be close to the kids and grandkids. What do I do? I received the recorder from Michelle yesterday and experimented with it, trying to get Brian's voice. The background noise was so strong that I did not get anything worthwhile. I will keep trying; I need to have his voice. It will comfort me later...

I am constantly trying to imagine my life without Brian. I suppose it is my way of preparing myself for the reality. How will I cope at his funeral? I am frightened of what my condition will be and of revealing the depth of my grief to others. I feel that I will cry and wail like a banshee. I would like to write something for the service, but I will be too emotional to read it out. Maybe I could put something on tape?...

Brian's pain, and the management of it, continued to dominate my days. Constant monitoring was necessary to maintain the level of control we had achieved. I was not to know that far better control was possible through the expertise of the pain management specialist attached to the Palliative Care Team, or how much our lives were to be enriched because of it.

Sometimes

Sometimes during the day I can shut my grief away

And concentrate on things to make him smile

We fish in the sun ... try to have some fun

Forget we have no future for a while

But when day turns to night and the house is quiet

I hear his laboured breathing by my side

Then my defenses crash down   and I try not to make a sound

As I lie beside my loved one and cry

Fear

Oh for the joy of sleeping peacefully
and waking with a light heart
Oh for the time when there were no tears
When laughter was not out of place and smiles came easy
Now those simple joys are gone
Good sleep is rare and nightmares reign
We wake in fear of pain unknown
My love to face his end so near
And me the loneliness to come … I fear

Pat leaves on Saturday ... I told her of my decision to sell the house and possibly move to Mandurah. She was enthusiastic and said, "Lorraine, you cannot live without hope, so it is good that you plan for the future." Her words meant the world to me. I am so grateful for her wisdom and the comfort she gives me. I feel better now that I have made these decisions. I know that nothing will be easy and it will hurt to leave our home and all the trees and plants, but I am not going to waste whatever time I have left on this earth away from my children. I will have my memories wherever I go.

I feel strange. When I leave the house everything is surreal; I don't want to be out for long, I hate crowds and I am finding it almost impossible to stay outwardly calm when Brian is getting worse. I know I will have to go to Perth to nurse him. I need emotional nursing myself. I try not to burden the children with my grief but I have to speak to someone and Pat is remarkable; we can talk about anything. It will be good to be close to her. I will also be able to contact hospice. They are trained for situations like this.

Sometimes when Brian is unable to swallow I think, this is it, and I am frozen with fear and dread; my stomach turns and I am helpless. Is this what I will be like when he is dying in front of my eyes? I pray that I don't have to see him go but if I am not there to hold him and say goodbye I will never get over it. I am so unhappy. The disease is starting to wear him down and witnessing his decline is wearing me down. There is nowhere to hide, nowhere to escape even for a little while. It is so cruel. I wish it would go away and then I feel terrible because it can only go away when he dies and I don't want him to die. I wish I could crawl into his arms and lie there forever...

We have been to Perth for a wedding and caught up with all the rellies, I had looked forward to the trip but when I got there I could not wait to come home. Normal life is foreign and uncomfortable for me. I feel much better now that I am home. Brian is more relaxed and his pain is back under control. Pat is with us and, as always, it is good to have her around ... Jules has made it through to the Pop Stars finals, a ray of sunshine in our bleak world.

One of the most tragic and upsetting symptoms of Brian's disease resulted from tumour growth pressing against his oesophagus; this narrowed the opening and made it almost impossible for him to swallow. He loved his food and it was terrible to see him lose his enjoyment of it, especially because, for a time, his appetite was good.

Dilatations (stretching of his oesophagus) allowed him to swallow some solid food, but most of it needed to be pureed and its appearance failed to tempt his eye or his palate. Many times when he tried to eat meat or fish it caught in his throat and I found myself chewing my own food into a pulp, willing him to swallow.

When he began to have difficulty taking his tablets I requested that his doctor prescribe Kapinol. These slow-release morphine capsules can be broken open and the contents sprinkled onto ice-cream. Brian found the ice-cream easy to swallow and I was able to continue giving him his medication orally. After checking with his doctor I crushed the various pills he took for symptom control and gave them to him in the same way.

CHEMOTHERAPY:

In time, Brian's condition worsened until he could not even drink water. Dilatations were no longer an option and he was offered palliative chemotherapy to shrink the tumour. It was the only hope of prolonging his life.

Like many before him, Brian had vowed that he would not undergo chemotherapy. Having heard stories of chronic fatigue, nausea, and hair loss he was fearful of the treatment. But there is a lot of truth in the adage, "You never know, until it happens to you". For Brian, where there was life, there was hope, and any means of prolonging that hope he grasped with both hands.

We were to remain in Perth for the duration of the chemotherapy sessions and, once again, John came to our rescue. He offered to take care of Ben and look after our house and garden in our absence.

Today the oncologist told Brian that the chemo would be given to him as a trial, in the hope it may shrink his tumour sufficiently to allow him to eat. There is a 40% chance that it will do nothing, other than make him extremely ill. Brian appears positive, though he must be terrified. Can I remain strong and encourage his belief that it will work, despite my doubts? ...

We have moved into Crawford Lodge. Everything has been provided for our needs. It is nice to look out at the bush and to hear the birds call in the mornings, hard to believe that the hospital is only a short walk away ...

Sitting in a chemotherapy ward as a patient or as a carer is an experience not to be forgotten. Cancer has no respect for gender, age, or wealth. There are people of every race, color, and creed; rich, middle class, and poor; and none of this makes the slightest difference. They are all united in their suffering, fellow human beings on the same sad journey. I was always thankful that the courage and determination of Brian and his fellow patients was met with the respect, compassion, cheerfulness, and efficiency of the staff.

Brian began his first round of chemotherapy in January 2001 with a combination of Cisplatin and Gemcitabine. His reaction was dramatic; he vomited continuously and needed to be hospitalized. As he was unable to retain anything orally, his medication was to be administered through injection. I provided the nurse with my journal - which clearly showed the medications he was on and their dosage - but he was not given the amount he relied on and, as a result, his pain intensified to seven on his pain scale.

The combination of continual nausea and uncontrolled pain, took a devastating toll on his physical and emotional wellbeing. To see him in pain knowing that I could not help him, upset me deeply. Outwardly I remained strong, but I was at a loss over what to do; Brian had surrendered himself to the system and I felt intrusive in his routine. Regardless, I did everything within my power to make him comfortable, scouting the hospital for an air mattress to relieve the pressure on the large swelling on his back and requesting extra pillows which I arranged, as I had at home, to aid his breathing. I remained with him for most of the days and late into the nights. Every time I left to walk down the long hospital corridor into the sunlight or the darkness of night, it felt symbolic of the journey I would travel without him. Every time the phone rang I feared that it was the hospital calling to say he was dying.

PALLIATIVE CARE:

Despite a terminal diagnosis, there is still life, and survival may range from months to several years. Many people believe that Palliative Care is intended only for the end of life, and do not seek their help until the final stages of terminal illness. Due to this unfortunate belief the quality of life that could have been achieved through their services is not realised.

The Palliative Care Team, consisting of pain management specialists, nurses, doctors, chaplains and volunteers, work together, to provide the best possible pain and symptom control for the patient, whilst at the same time offering physical and emotional support to their families. I believe the services of these wonderful people should be embraced from the time of terminal diagnosis. Had Brian been in their care sooner, much of his suffering, and mine, would have been alleviated.

My meeting with them happened by chance, when I took a different route from Brian's ward, and came upon their office. Looking back I believe that the hand of an angel led me to them as from the moment I began to speak, I realised I had at last found someone who understood what I was going through. It was such a relief to unburden my fears and, though my tears continued to flow, their understanding and compassion comforted me.

We discussed the medication Brian was on prior to admission and my concerns regarding his current pain. They wasted no time in conferring with the oncology staff who adjusted his medication accordingly. Eventually, to our immense relief, Brian's pain was brought under control. His nausea, however, took longer to abate; he became weak from lack of food and nourishment and lost a total of eight kilos. Placed on a drip, he remained in hospital for several days.

During his stay, methadone was introduced into his pain management; it was hoped that this, used in conjunction with hydromorphone for break through pain, would remove his need for large doses of kapinol and become his staple means of pain control.

Tonight I went up to a stranger, sitting with others outside a ward where a loved one was dying, and hugged her. I told her that I understood what she was going through. Seeing her sad vigil made me even more determined that Brian would die at home...

We have moved in with Pat and Noel and will stay here until the next treatment. It is good to be free of the confines of the hospital with all its disease, death, and sadness. The lodge is excellent but I have missed a home environment. Pat is amazing; I don't know what I would do without her ... Being in Perth is good. I can see the kids and my family often. Ben is now with us and Clint has brought my computer down but it is impossible to enjoy anything for any length of time. There is no hope of a cure, no hope of a future for Brian and me, no hope of anything... It is hard not being in control of my life, my days, my possessions. Life has become an existence, day-in, day-out, trying to bear the pain, trying to remain strong, trying to convince myself that I will survive. I miss my own home, my own routine and my comforts around me ... but I do not miss Exmouth.

Brian's first round of chemo is almost over. I dread going back home; I am afraid that I will not be able to cope there any longer. It upsets me that Brian does not understand my turmoil. His friends keep telling me that he loves Exmouth and I should not make him leave. What makes them think I am not aware of his love of the place? They have no comprehension of what I am going through … This morning I woke full of anxiety and had difficulty breathing. I told Brian about my fears, I had to. I could no longer ignore the condition I was in. I know how much he wants to stay, and it saddens me, but I will need help if I am to continue to support him through this ordeal.

Today Brian had major sweats all day. I am worried about what this means. He is also having more cramps on his left side. Apart from this he has been remarkably good. It is wonderful that his appetite has returned and he is able to enjoy some variety in his meals. Pat cooks lamb shanks in the pressure cooker and they are so tender that he is able to chew and swallow the meat without difficulty. When he appears well his impending death is harder to bear. Someone less informed may think that because he appears to be better, he is better. I have no such illusions; I live in constant fear that I could lose him at any time. Does he still hope that through some miracle he will beat this? Maybe he does. It would be impossible to get up each day with the thought of dying.

God help me, it's getting harder. Brian looks so frail. Every time I look at him I feel such sadness. I miss everything we once had. I miss Brian, my strong beautiful man, I miss life. I miss hope. I am terrified of his death and equally terrified of my life without him...

Shortly after leaving hospital the benefits of methadone become obvious. For the first time since diagnosis, there were periods of time during which Brian felt no pain. This, and his ability to sleep through the night, dramatically improved his wellbeing. Slow-release capsules were no longer necessary and as his methadone was taken at eight-hourly intervals, it allowed us more freedom.

As the tumour continued to grow it began to crush his surrounding organs causing his pain to break through his medication. Hydromorphone almost always gave speedy relief and we continued it until, following consultation with his doctors, his methadone dose was increased. In this way we achieved remarkable pain control, far better than many thought possible considering the nature of Brian's disease. There were days when he experienced no pain at all and this was wonderful.

For the second round of chemotherapy, Brian was given Gemcitabene on its own; this was much kinder to his system and did not result in nausea. The third round, however, was to be the same combination as the first; and after his ordeal, Brian was loathe to undergo it again. The pain care specialist attached to the Palliative Care Team prescribed what he referred to as his "secret recipe"; two drugs, Haloperidol and Phenergan, to be taken on the night before, and in the morning, prior to treatment. He explained that both the brain and the gut are responsible for nausea and that Haloperidol controlled the message to the brain and Phenergan controlled the gut. Together, these two drugs worked so effectively that Brian never again suffered nausea due to his chemotherapy treatments.

Without fear of side effects, Brian welcomed his chemotherapy sessions and it was not long before its benefits became obvious. My views on chemotherapy changed as I realised that through it we had been given a gift of time. Accepting that the tumour would grow, and that further chemotherapy would follow, we decided to return to Exmouth for a short time before putting our home on the market and relocating to Perth.

Lorraine Kember

Precious Moments

There's laughter now in our days

For we have grown stronger

We have learned to push our grief away

And to live each moment

Of every single day

For we know that tomorrow may never come

And that our goodnight may well be our last goodbye

Brian has been amazing. There is no doubt that the chemotherapy has shrunk the tumour. He is able to eat meat and enjoy food again. I can't get over the change in him. He is so "normal", doing lots of things, out and about; calling into the pub every day for a few beers, visiting his mates, and going fishing. I am so grateful, but I wish he would take me with him. I am alone in the house with nothing to do and nowhere to go.

Today he went with Laurie to catch squid. He was away longer than he promised and I began to worry; his medication was due and he did not have it on him. When he finally came home I was upset and told him that I was not too flash when he is away from me. After giving me a quick hug, he left again to go down the street. I gave in to a huge cry. I am angry. My life is in constant turmoil. I see, hear, understand, and must bear it all. Am I angry because it appears that I am grieving more than he is? ...We don't do anything nice together any more. All I do is try to control his pain and watch him sleeping. He must see me as his nurse, the giver of medicine, and I think he is glad to get away from me sometimes ... I am happy for him to go to the pub for a bet and a drink with his mates but when I am alone reality sets in. I have no escape. I have no friends. Brian's friends worked with him; I barely know them. How can this be happening to us? He can't be dying. He can't be. He is so young. I am so young. Too young to be a widow.

Brian, my darling, my only love,

I cannot comprehend what it will be like when the thread between us is severed and I can no longer gaze at your beautiful face, share my thoughts with you, kiss you or just be with you. I must form some sort of plan for the future or I will not have the strength to decide in which direction I should go. My counsellor tells me not to worry about this but words mean nothing, they cannot control my emotions. I can only do my best and I believe I am doing well, though it is getting harder to cope with my grief...

I wish we could make love again. It's not fair that he can eat and drink and go fishing once more but cannot make love to me. I need him. I am so grateful for this gift of time but of course I long for the part of our marriage that we have lost. It is natural, it is allowed, and it is too big a loss not to mention.

Mum has told me to call her, day or night, if I need to talk; there are many nights when I lie awake in despair, but I don't pick up the phone. What is the point of phoning her? Or anyone? Why wake them up and burden them with my anxiety and grief when they can't say one word to make it go away or make me feel better? There are still times when I think I would rather die with him than live without him. When he holds me and I feel the solidness of him, the warmth of him, the feel of his skin and hair next to mine, I know that nothing will ever ease the pain of losing him...

We'll soon be living in Perth and I'm glad; it will good to be with the kids. We're looking for a house to rent near Clint and Dee; I will need their support even after Brian has died. He looks really sick lately. I half expect it to happen at any time, and as he gets worse, so do I. I'm not coping too well at the moment; I feel like I'm dying. I look terrible but I have no energy to do anything about it.

We have found a house but they have said "no animals"; I will write a letter about our circumstances. Ben is old and does not dig in the garden. Surely, if we give a dog bond and agree to leave him outside, they will let us have him. We are now in Exmouth packing up the house and I am exhausted. I watched Brian pack his beloved shell collection tonight and I could not help wondering if he will he ever unpack them. How does he feel right now? Does he think, like me, that he may never unpack his belongings? I have these thoughts often but I push them away. In my mind, I have been to the very depth of despair. I have imagined what it will be like when he dies. I do not need to dwell on it. I cannot change what is going to happen. Right now he is alive and I am determined to enjoy this precious time with him.

Well, here we are in Perth and our home is finally in some sort of order. Brian and I have had fun shopping, filling up two trolleys for $276.00, unheard of in Exmouth! It felt so normal, so good. Living in Perth, surrounded by life, is good for me. Dianne and Dennis popped in to see us today and again I *marvelled at the pleasure of being so close to the family. I feel like I am living now, not just sitting around waiting for it to happen.*

It is with wonder and gratitude that I write this on the night of Brian's birthday, a birthday I never thought he would be here for. We have had a great day with the kids and a special day is planned tomorrow with the rest of the family. It is so good to see the kids regularly; I will never place myself so far away from them again...

Today Brian went out with Clint and came home with a Jack Russel puppy. He is so cute. We have called him Rufus.

At times Dexamethasone was added to Brian's pain management program; this increased his appetite and gave him energy. He loved to walk around the shops and we did this for several hours each day.

At night, he was reluctant to sleep and would stay up late either studying the race form or working on one of his hobbies. He was very creative and made a beautiful pendant, cut from pearl shell, for each of the women in our family; he also painted didgeridoos. I loved to see him relax in this way, but since his skin had become thin, he bruised easily and, fearing for his safety, I could not go to bed until he did. Eventually I became exhausted, dragging myself around the shops with no heart for any of our purchases.

I have felt rotten all day, irritable, fat, dizzy, and vague. I worry about my own health. I am so bloody tired. Why can't we have a day or two without having to do anything? I am angry, too; it is hard seeing Brian look well but knowing it won't last. There is no joy in our life anymore; a house needs life and plans and hopes for the future and we have none of these things.

I realised today that it is Brian's life I am living; I am so consumed with his wants and needs that I have no emotional or physical energy left over to nurture myself. Small breaks away from the house would be good for me, and everyone has offered to help, but I cannot leave him. I am so afraid that I will come home to find him dead. Tonight, he said to me, "I am aggravated. Perhaps we should go on a trip but I am afraid to spend so much money when I might still be around in ten years time". It broke my heart to hear him talk this way. It was all I could do to stop myself from saying the words that screamed in my head, "You are dying! You will not be here in ten years, or even five. What is to become of me? I am so frightened. I miss you and I miss the person I used to be". But I can't say these things to my beautiful man. He humbles me with his courage and I must dig deep to find my own so that I can remain strong for him. He must never know that I have no hope of his survival.

I am so glad we have Rufus, he has given us something to focus on and his antics make us laugh. For a little dog, he has such character and is quick to learn. Brian loves him and it is wonderful to see his enjoyment. Ben has a new lease of life, endlessly playing with him and looking after him like a parent, his gentleness is amazing.

Rufus and Ben

Tonight we went to see Julie sing with her new band. I dressed up for the first time in ages and it felt so good to be out. But the crowded room and loud music disturbed Brian and we left shortly after. I really felt the difference between us. The music made me feel alive and I longed to abandon myself to it and the joy of hearing Julie sing. I could have stayed to the bitter end, jumping around on the dance floor with the rest of them.

Julie - *centre in the Blush Band*

We have been talking about buying our own house and have even looked at a few - this brings back the heartache and uselessness of it all. What ever we choose, it will only be me who lives in it. I don't know how I will be, or where I will want to live, a few years down the track. We really should not be buying at all. Brian is hell bent on it. I think he is anxious to have everything set up so that I will be alright financially when he is gone. I am so grateful for this time we have had together, far beyond the doctor's prediction. Brian buys me flowers often and holds my hand and hugs me, even in public. Our caresses say what we are feeling but cannot put into words. They say, I don't want you to die. I am frightened. Hold me. Hold me tight and never let me go … He told me today that our thirty two years of marriage deserved a long service ring. I said a ring would be nice, but that I thought it should be called a "devotion ring". I hope he buys one for me, it would be such a lovely thing to cherish …

Brian grows increasingly more tired and sometimes falls asleep in the middle of talking to me. This morning it upset me so much that I cried and told him that I wanted him back. I don't like to upset him by breaking down this way but I am not super woman and I needed him to comfort me, a luxury I can no longer take for granted…

In July 2001, just five months prior to his death, Brian expressed a wish to go on a men's only fishing trip to Exmouth.

I don't want Brian to go to Exmouth without me, but I have to let him go. He needs to be "one of the boys". I pray that he is well enough to enjoy it. I am terrified that he will not return to me. But so many times I have feared the worst and it has not happened. His magnificent heart is still beating. How much longer can he hold death at bay? Fifteen days is too long for us to be apart. Please God, bring him back to me alive.

Brian is now in Exmouth. I am constantly projecting myself into the future, deliberately torturing myself: looking at his photos, the flowers he has planted, his car, his room, his treasures. I think I am preparing myself for his death. How will I endure it? I am so frightened...

Michelle, Clint and Dee are ill with a new strain of flu. I am worried for them and Jules; this flu is killing people. I will probably get it too. What if Brian does? It is a quarter past ten and I have realised that it is not good for me to be on my own for twenty-four hours. I have been willing the time away, waiting for Brian to call. He sounded really good. I am happy for him but it hurts that he does not need me. I miss him even though I get so tired trying to keep up with him. We should not be apart for so long. I feel lost; it is hard to know what to do when, for nineteen months, everything I have done is for him. I need him. I feel so alone...

Missing You

You've been gone so long and my heart has been blue

I've seen so clearly what it will be like without you

The house is so quiet - just the two dogs and me

I wait for your calls every night - they reassure me

But what do I do when you can no longer call?

What will I do when I can't reach you at all?

How will I stop myself thinking of you

Remembering our love in all that I do?

How will I live for the rest of my life

without the feeling that I'm still your wife?

How will I find a reason to go on

When you - my reason for living - has gone?

I have not written for ages, I have not felt the need. I have found a house I like. Brian has told me to put an offer on it. I can't wait for him to come home. Tonight is the last night on my own. I have done a lot of soul-searching in his absence and realise that I will be okay. I read back through my diary and I can see how far I have come. I am so much stronger than I was; I have faced the future without him and accepted that I will survive. Somewhere deep inside there is the Lorraine I once knew. I only hope that I can find her, once this tragedy is over …

Not long after Brian returned from his holiday in Exmouth he again experienced trouble swallowing. This, and other symptoms, indicated that the tumour had grown dramatically and was pressing against his oesophagus. Tragically his enjoyment of food was once more taken from him.

Yesterday Ben was bitten by a tiger snake in our back yard. I couldn't believe it. I always feared this in Exmouth but not here. I rushed him to the vet and the wait to see if he would survive was terrible.

Brian had not had a good day and my added anxiety over Ben put my emotions on overload. I shut myself in my room, curled into a tight ball on the floor, and sobbed my heart out. Against all odds, Ben pulled through. His survival has been a miracle; why can't we find one for Brian?

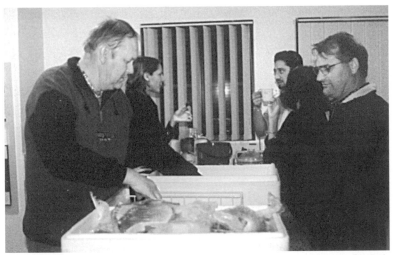

Brian and Dennis *(foreground) splitting the catch after returning from holiday in Exmouth*

On the weekend, we were given a wonderful gift. Michelle, with Pat's help, had contacted all our family and friends and together they raised over $3,500 for us to go on a trip to Darwin. It was a total surprise and we are overwhelmed … We leave on Monday; I am looking forward to it but I am worried that Brian will deteriorate while we are away. He almost always has trouble getting food down and meal times fill me with apprehension. I don't know how he manages to carry on and be so uncomplaining when inside he must be screaming, why me? Why me?

We got back from Darwin today. It is so good to be home. I need to talk to someone and have a good cry. Brian has struggled to eat every day; it was hard seeing this and not being able to speak of it to anyone or even write in my diary. Most of the time he was too sick to do anything, but there were some good times, some nice memories to keep. We enjoyed the jumping crocodiles and the beautiful botanical gardens. But most of all, the sunset cruise, where we stood together on the deck and watched the first stars come into the sky. I will always remember the feel of his arms around me as I lent against him and the overwhelming sadness I felt knowing that our time together is almost over. I began to cry and he said, "Don't cry, it will be alright". I have never loved him more than at that moment.

Today, I came out to find Brian with his head on the table and his arms hanging by his side and thought he'd died. Watching this happen to him has made me fearful of my own and my children's mortality. I am afraid of having to bear this terrible pain again …

I don't know where to start. Yesterday New York was attacked by terrorists and as we watched the devastation on TV I felt sick. Thousands of lives are lost. The threat of war has increased my turmoil. Will there be terrorist attacks here? What will happen to me and the kids? Brian will not be here to protect us … I am weakening, I feel panic coming on, I ache to scream. I make so many unconscious noises; it is the tension leaking out of me but it needs to pour out, it is suffocating me with its weight.

The kids are suffering with the strain of witnessing Brian's decline and I believe they are also worried about me. I am tired of all this pain. I want to wake up with the thought of life, not death, but it will be a long time before this is possible. When Brian dies I will still wake with the thought of death. But it will be reality, not expectation. Oh God, what terrible knowledge this is. No one can give him back to me. I miss him so much already, there is so little of the Brian that was ... I feel like I am falling into a sea of nothingness. I am so tired; the impending move is too much for me. Brian can't do much of anything and I don't know where to start. Last night, after writing in my diary, I could not stop crying; Brian held me as best he could and told me over and over how much he loved me.

Well, we have finally moved in, and I am exhausted... The family was marvelous; they worked all day and did not leave us until everything was in place. It is now four in the morning, but I cannot sleep. I keep thinking about how much joy the house could bring us if Brian was well. Soon it will only be me between the walls.

We have spent another half day at the shopping centre. I tried hard to be enthusiastic but by the time we got home I felt exhausted. This afternoon Brian asked me to work in the garden. I have carted bags of potting mix, manure, and mulch, planted two trees, and what seemed like a hundred onions. Brian watched everything I did and became quite critical, telling me how deep to dig the holes, which way to put the plants in, and how to rake the soil around them. I know it frustrates him that he can no longer garden himself but trying to do everything and be everything he needs is sometimes more than I can manage. My back is killing me...

Today we went to the doctor. It was as bad as I feared. Brian was told quite bluntly that there is nothing to save him. They spoke of more chemo but warned that this could

93

not go on indefinitely... It is no longer possible to put a needle into the veins in his arms. A port has been put into his chest; at least this will save him some discomfort. We are both struggling to remain calm. I ache for him. I ache for myself. How much longer will this nightmare go on? I have a strong premonition of two months. I don't know why.

Yesterday Brian was admitted to hospital with dehydration. This did not surprise me; he has not been able to swallow much of anything. I again managed to get him an air mattress. It is so different to the last time he was in; the Palliative Care Team are looking after him and I can relax knowing that he is comfortable and free of pain. The doctors have decided to put a stent into his oesophagus. Hopefully this will push the tumour aside enough to allow him to swallow. They have told me that, due to the weight of the tumour, the stent will not last long. I dread to think of the implications of this. I don't know from one day to next if it will be his last.

Brian and Me - *November 2001*

So much has happened since I last wrote. Brian is not strong enough to endure further chemotherapy. I feel raw. What has this news done to him? The stent is in place but he has lost all interest in food. Yesterday we brought him home from hospital but he had trouble breathing and went back in the ambulance. He is now on oxygen. I have arranged for an air compressor, oxygen bottles, and a wheel chair to be delivered to the house. Tomorrow I will work out a roster with Michelle, Julie, and Pat, and arrange for the Silver Chain nurse to call daily. I want to have everything in place so that Brian can come home. I am determined that he will not die in hospital.

I woke this morning with dread, as usual, the heaviness of my spirit overwhelming me before I even begin the day. It is as terrible as I imagined. Brian is so weak he can hardly walk and needs oxygen most of the time. He is fighting to live and I can't help but wonder what he is fighting for. We all put on our brave faces and try to be strong for each other. We have been busy fixing the fence, washing the cars, and buying a new one. It is far from a house of impending death. There is much noise, life. It is surreal but I will remember always that we did achieve a sense of normality for Brian even in the face of such despair ...

Brian's extremities are shutting down; there is only a shell of him left, he is helpless. I push his wheelchair, go into public toilets with him, and appear to be calm, but I am not. I am in control. The steel cage is in place. He knows he is dying. I can't imagine what thoughts and fears he has; he does not mention them to me.

It is reassuring to have someone here, but at times I long for my own space, my own routine, and some private time with Brian. He has told me that my haste flusters him, causing him to become breathless. I must school myself to move slowly and be quiet around him; this will not be easy, I am not a quiet person by nature. It is devastating to see the disease taking him from me. I have helped him live even in the shadow of death; I have made it possible for him to die at home surrounded by his loved ones. I cannot do any more ...

Brian seems alright at the moment; I have told Michelle and Pat to have a few days off. It must be like a life raft for them to go back to their loved ones and experience a household free of impending death. I am weak from giving. I need. I need. My love is as strong as ever but my body, my heart, and my soul feel empty ...

We drove to the Rose Garden Nursery today and, for the short time Brian was awake, he loved it. Pat and I make a terrific team. We manage to get the wheelchair, oxygen, medicine, and all of the other things Brian needs into the car and get him out of the house, allowing him to see things of beauty and be still amongst the living.

It is tiring and the anxiety of making sure that he is okay is draining but I get strength doing this for him. He now accepts that he is dying, but he never complains nor loses his beautiful smile. I am awed by his courage. I wish that I could lie beside him, feel his arms around me, and just melt right into him. I still sometimes wish that I could go with him ... I can't imagine ever not hurting with all the memories. God help me. Help me to bear the grief that is rushing towards me.

Pat told me today that Brian is worried about me. I suppose it would be strange if he were not. I am okay, at least for the moment I am fairly calm and accepting of this progression. I want peace for him - for all of us. When the end does come, I think I will be okay...

December is here again. We have done the Christmas shopping. Pat and I took Brian and his wheelchair to the shopping centre. It was crowded but he enjoyed it. We selected the children's gifts together and then he sent me off so that he and Pat could buy something for me ... He even selected the goodies for the dinner table. It was heartbreaking to see his enthusiasm knowing that he would not be able to eat any of it ... It is his dearest wish to be with us on Christmas Day; he keeps asking me what the date is, and I know that with sheer determination, he is holding death at bay...

Lorraine Kember

Prescious Time

You may be vague and asleep in your chair

But my darling - you are still there

Our time is so prescious even when you are sleeping

I take in your face for my sad future's keeping

But the pain takes the pleasure of you being near

I know there'll be peace in what we both fear...

Believing

I have to believe there's another place
beyond this world we know
So that when your time on earth is done
you have a place to go…
I have to believe - you'll wait for me
and that I will find you home
I have to believe - so that I can bear
this life once I'm alone
I pray that we will meet again
because our love will never die
Surely there's another world
a time for you and I…

Death

It waits in the shadows but it sneaks ever closer

I can sense it - almost smell it - tangible - real - waiting

Death - it waits like a vulture - watching the once strong body falter

But it has no notion of will - the will to live - which fights on

refusing to see death - even though it stares him in the face

It does not honour courage

But I - witness to this brave struggle

Will forever hold my love in awe

His courage humbles me - his uncomplaining nature humbles me

and his love - unchanging and ever true - holds me up

We have spoken of death. I asked Brian if he was frightened and he said, "No, it will be nice to sleep". We spoke of his parents and the hope that they would be waiting for him. When he asked me about his funeral, I told him of my plans for a seaside memorial. He was pleased with my decision. I have remained strong and I believe I am helping Brian to die well, just as I have helped him to live for these past two years. It comforts me that he is not afraid of dying. He knows that his long courageous battle is almost over; he has accepted it and is at peace.

Brian's health has deteriorated dramatically, he is now unable to leave his bed. Christmas is only three days away, but I don't think he can hold on much longer. Since our talks there is a deep peacefulness within me and, for the most part, I am calm about his impending death. I do not want to see his continued suffering. I am so thankful that I have remained strong and able to help him ... I pray that he goes peacefully...

We have moved his bed into the family room so that he can observe life going on around him and remain an important part of it. Michelle, Clint, Julie and Pat are with us. We spend every precious moment with Brian supporting him physically and emotionally with our love...

On Monday morning 24th December 2001,two years after diagnosis, Brian's courageous battle with mesothelioma came to an end – he was fifty-four years old.

Goodbye

I stood at your bedside

held your hand - let you know

That the children and I were okay

you could go

You peacefully left us

no longer in pain

I told you I loved you - again and again

I held your dear body

In my arms one last time

I'll never forget you

Loved husband of mine

It was such a relief that Brian's suffering was over; he looked so peaceful. The wrench of it, the terrible sadness is indescribable, yet I feel peace. We had a wonderful and abiding love. I would not wish him back to the state he was in or my anguish to see him so. Pat helped me dress him and we gave him a shave; in all our years together I had never done that. I supported his body in my arms, truly held him one last time. He looked beautiful. I kissed him often and told him over and over that I loved him. Pat kissed him too, and each time she did, I kissed him again, wanting my kiss to be the last to go with him ...

I am glad that he died at home; he stayed with us for a long time ... We picked a bunch of flowers from the garden, placed them on his chest, and put photos and tokens in his pocket. Clint put a can of beer in his hand and said, "Go catch a big one, Macka". To my dying day I will be grateful for the strength I was granted and the help I received which made it possible for me to make Brian's death as loving, sharing, and peaceful as anyone could wish for. I know that this helped our children to deal with the terrible loss of their beloved father. This knowledge holds me up.

I have been casting my mind back over the last few days... For some reason, I desperately need to know what we did... Friday I wheeled him out onto the patio; I rocked in the hammock while he sat in his chair and he told me that he loved looking at the garden. Later, we went inside and played a few games of dice. He won most of them. Saturday, he suddenly became very ill and was unable to leave his bed. On Sunday, we realised that he would not be with us for Christmas, so we gathered around him and exchanged our presents. He was fully conscious. He took my hand and placed a beautiful ring on my finger... He had not forgotten our conversation. My devotion ring - his last loving gift to me - I will treasure forever...

With Brian's death we lost a loving husband, father, grandfather, brother, uncle, son in law, nephew and friend. He touched the lives of many; and we are blessed for the privilege of having known and loved him.

Brian and I travelled many miles on our last journey together. Miles of emotions, spirits, courage and strength. I thanked God for granting me the courage and the strength to walk beside him to his life's end and for the peace I found in the knowledge that I *definitely* made a difference.

Back to the Bay

Sleep peacefully my love until you find your wings

Then glide to where your dreams abide

where your paradise awaits

Endless time to search the shore for shells

Mud crabs wait in every hole

and the mangrove jacks are jumping

The net is full - the beer is cold

And the Toyota is parked at the Bay

THE MEMORIAL:

Tomorrow is the day of Brian's funeral; I have planned each step with the same calm that has prevailed since he died. But now that all the planning is done, I feel strange. I look at his wheelchair and the oxygen compressor, now on the front porch waiting to be collected,   and I can so clearly see him, determined to enjoy his life even though all the things he loved except for his family, had been taken from him. I see myself too, standing behind him, protecting him, loving him, determined to help him live and to help him die when the time came. I miss him so much. I see him everywhere. It doesn't matter how many times I tell myself that his spirit is at the Bay of Rest, I know that he, the man I have loved, protected, and cherished above all others, is about to be cremated. God help me ...

We chose a grassy knoll overlooking the ocean for the memorial; Clint strung Brian's fishing net around the area. It felt so right to see it there. The sun created a shimmer over the crystal clear water as, together with family and friends, I looked out over this beautiful vista and said farewell to Brian.

Julie's beautiful song, and special words written and recorded by Michelle and myself, were played, followed by eulogies from two dear friends, evoking laughter, as well as tears, when many of Brian's fishing exploits were recalled. The album we provided with photographs of family and friends throughout the years was welcomed by all. It came as no surprise that fish in one form or another featured in most of them.

After the ceremony, in true Brian tradition, we lit up the barbecue for a sausage sizzle, enjoyed a few tinnies and listened to his favorite Slim Dusty tunes. It was a beautiful and uplifting service, a wonderful tribute to Brian's memory. I believe many saw it as a gift, a special opportunity to feel close to him and I was so glad I had followed my instincts. My children, strong like me, welcomed everyone and thanked them for coming. Brian would have been so proud of us.

The Funeral

The car moved slowly - you within

your favorite flowers above

Closed in a wooden coffin

my worst nightmare come true

I walked behind you - saw you in my mind

and cried my anguish

I wanted to rip the lid off

reach in and hold you

tell you that I loved you

and that I was with you still

Could you feel my pain

I needed so desperately to see you again

Then I carried you - laid you down

heard the piper play

and had to leave you there

Part of my heart I left beside you

It will never beat the same again.

Dreaming

I wonder - is death like dreaming when your body is left behind

and your spirit - free to wander - sends pictures to your mind?

Is it just a pleasant interlude when a body cannot hold

the soul it once protected because it's sick or old?

Is death then eternal - or are we reborn?

Do we become a gift of life - or take another form?

Will we become a breath of air - a flower - a brook - a tree

Or are there endless choices for a soul set free to be?

I hope that you are dreaming - your spirit strong and free

And that when my time on earth is done

You'll wake and call to me

THE QUESTION OF PROGNOSIS:

A prognosis is an estimation, calculated on other people's experiences, and is often inaccurate. Many patients live far longer than predicted and achieve things they never thought possible.

Brian's survival of two years, despite his prognosis of three to nine months, has strengthened my belief that no one can accurately predict how long a person might survive - because every one of us is unique.

Each terminal patient, though on the same journey, may not travel at the same speed, take the same turns in the road, or reach the end of the road at the same time as those who have travelled before them.

Prognosis brings with it the tendency to "count down" until the expected time of demise. This has a huge impact on the quality of day-to-day life; many die at or around the time of prediction, simply because they were told to.

I believe that a prognosis should be given to the patient only if requested. There are many who ask for an estimation so they can put their affairs in order. I suspect there are an equal number who do not, choosing instead to live in the hope of recovery.

Whether or not a prognosis is given to the patient, the carer, by necessity, must be in acceptance of a terminal diagnosis. It is extremely difficult to maintain an appearance of hope for your loved one whilst at the same time coping with your grief in anticipation of their death. It is painful to hear them talk of hopes and dreams for the future, knowing that they may not be realised. However, it is this very hope that brings purpose into their lives and helps them to endure the ravages of the disease. This often results in longer survival, and if only one of their dreams is realised, it is a wonderful achievement.

MY JOURNEY:

The two years of suffering I endured in anticipation of Brian's death had, in a sense, prepared me for it. I had already suffered many of the stages of grief and overcome them. I no longer had anger. I was in acceptance of his death. There was no guilt. There was nothing left that I wished I could have said or done - I said and did it all during his illness.

The life I had known for almost thirty-seven years had come to an end. My children, family and relations returned to their partners, their families, and their hopes and dreams for the future. It was strange to be alone; emptiness was everywhere. I no longer had Brian - or anyone - at home to share my life with. I was alone, in every sense of the word, and frightened of what the future had in store for me.

I have begun waking early each morning, my mind instantly on Brian, going over and over his death. I see his face so clearly and remember the feel of his skin; firm, unyielding, strange. I wish I could have been alone with him for awhile, but I may have lost complete control and that would not have been good for me or for the others and perhaps even Brian. Maybe he was still with us in spirit. Even after he died I tried to remain strong - for him and for the children. I do not have to be strong anymore...

I cannot relax, yet when I begin a task, I do not have the mental or physical energy to complete it. I can't seem to focus on anything. I have not done any housework - can't seem to start or finish anything bar the watering, but I understand ... The children tell me they are the same. It is grief. It will wave over us. I am okay. I recognise it and just let myself be. The housework will wait ...

111

I crave quiet. I see Brian everywhere and cry a million tears for my loss. I have placed his toothbrush next to mine, wear his pyjamas to bed, and play memories of him over and over in my mind. The nights are the worst; despite my incredible tiredness I find it hard to sleep and when I do, it is restless and broken with dreams. Many times I wake up crying. I have begun sitting in his place at the table and in his recliner, even sitting where he died, calling him, and hoping by some miracle that I can feel his presence.

Time passes relentlessly and I carry on alone, missing Brian more than words can say. I often talk aloud to him because I need to say his name. Looking at his photos brings a sense of unreality, feelings that it can't be true. Yet even as I form the thought, I know it is true. He is dead. He will not come back to me ever again.

There's no gold at the end of my rainbow
No dream that will ever come true
No wish that could ever be granted
That could take the place of you...

It is Michelle's birthday today; we went to the casino. I stood at the wheel of fortune and could hardly believe that Brian will never bet on it again. He has been gone for five days now; I continue to be strong, I do enjoy the day, the beautiful garden, the freedom to come and go...but it is surreal. I constantly search for memories, reliving them, missing him.

My Darling,

It is just one week since your funeral. It seems longer. I feel like you have been gone for ages. I miss you. I'm hungry for the sight of you, the sound of you, and the feel of you. I wish you could somehow reach me. Are you looking down on me as I write?

Sadness has settled on me like a cloak. I keep remembering things he said, things he did. I think about his love of food and cooking before the disease took the enjoyment from him. I think about his love of plants. I see him in every plant I tend. Every time I water the garden I hear him telling me not to forget the peach tree, or to nip the heads off the dead petunias, often saying his words aloud and smiling at the memory. So many times I think, I must tell Brian this, show him that. And then I remember that I can never tell or show him anything ever again. Julie went to Tamworth and had her song, "A Moment in Time", played on the radio in his memory. He would have been so proud of her...

Julie - *Our little song bird - Tamworth 2002*

Twenty Four Days

Only twenty four days since you've been gone

Yet it seems so long - so long

Since I saw your face

Heard your voice

Watched you smile

Rubbed your back - held your hand

for a while

Twenty four days since you've been gone

I want you back

You've been gone too long

It is a strange world I find myself in ... odd one out, don't seem to fit or be comfortable anywhere. I feel as if I am alone in a small boat, without oars, on a very rough ocean. I hate living on my own yet when I am out I want to come home again. My house protects me like a blanket. I must be careful not to let it smother me. I must stop pawing over photos of Brian. It is making me weak and I must remain strong. He is gone. I cannot bring him back; I must seek new friends and develop a new life though I hardly want to. Life without Brian is empty, so long has he been a part of me. I am so achingly lonely ...

It is now six weeks since Brian died - forty two days - it seems so much longer. I feel vulnerable and increasingly angry and frustrated by my lack of physical strength. It is hard to do all the man things around the house and garden. There are some things I simply cannot do, I am not a man after all.

My Darling
Without you I am like a small child learning to walk. I take a few steps and I falter, needing your hand to guide me. I achieve something and I miss your praise. I stumble and I miss you being there to comfort me and hold me up with your love. Around me, everyone has a partner, a lover, and I am jealous. I look at your photos and can't believe that you are dead. It feels like you are away on a holiday. It is time you came home. If only this had all been a bad dream and I could wake up one day and find you beside me. I miss you so...

115

It is strange to have so much time on my hands. I spend hours in the garden; it feels good to be tending the plants Brian loved. I remember the many times we went to the nursery to select them. He used to say, "Don't rush, let's walk down every aisle". I listened to his voice on tape; it was good to hear him call me "darl" and to hear him laugh. I am glad I thought to do this. I have had the little heart he gave me set into his wedding ring and I wear it on a chain around my neck. It comforts me.

I continue to be strong, I miss Brian - but I do not miss the anxiety, the fear, and the knowledge of impending death. It is good to go to bed and not be afraid of what awaits me in the morning. But I am lonely; it is not good to be on my own night after night. So many people have been with me over the past two years and now there is no one. Part of me enjoys the solitude - but not endless solitude. I will have to join some clubs, make friends, and find a purpose for my life. Tonight I keep seeing Brian in his chair, in his wheelchair, everywhere. I still sit in his chair every night; I am drawn to it. I am always trying to feel his presence ...

Alone

I am so lonely - since you've been gone

My empty house yawns

The dogs rouse to greet me - my silent companions

I put the kettle on, put one cup on the sink

Sit alone at a table for six

Imagine you in your chair

I smile, but you are not there

I plan the day - and do nothing

Watch videos of you and me

Freeze frame us as we danced

Hungry for you, I play the tape again and again

I want to reach into the screen - grab you

Place you beside me

I have ventured out into the world again. Last night I went to a Life Changing Seminar, which will run for another few weeks. Hopefully it will help me find direction in my life. Today I took a MYOB computer course. I enjoyed the stimulation and the company. I felt happy when I got home but now as always the loneliness is with me. I miss sharing my experiences with Brian. It is hard to endure the transition from a married woman to a widow. I must now make all of the decisions; there is no one who will truly look out for me. I stand alone in a crowd of couples and hear them say - my wife - my husband. I have no husband, I am no longer a wife, I am alone…

Not Like That

I want you back - but not like that - the memory is too clear

Of pain - nausea and heartache added to the fear

I mourned for you along the way as we lost our joy of life

And couldn't share the intimacy we deserved as man & wife

We couldn't plan for anything so we lived just for the day

But it was hard to pretend that all was well

when our thoughts got in the way

It is still so clear - the thought of you - so sick - so weak - so strong

I still feel anger that you died so young - it's wrong

I want you back - but not like that

I want you as before - my strong but tender lover

I'll remember ever more.

I sat and looked through the photo albums again this morning; pictures of Brian from a boy right through to Michelle's wedding. It made me cry. This afternoon I felt better; went shopping and went berserk, bought a heap of new clothes. It felt good! I need to take a bit of pride in myself. I am going to lose weight ... I miss Brian terribly but I am okay. I have grown so much, I have a lot to give, and God willing, I will keep my health and find a new life. I deserve it. I am proud of the way I helped Brian. I am rewarded by my strength and my determination to live my life to the fullest. I thank the goodness out there for my many blessings...

Michelle and Mark are good to me. Tonight they took me to tea but I missed Brian so much. All I wanted was to cry. I wish with all my heart that I could have him back. I am not really as strong as I thought ...

Somewhere on a distant shore
I'll find your footprints in the sand
And just around the corner
You'll be there to take my hand ...

Tonight I feel sad, angry and lonely. I sat around all day achieving nothing. There is plenty to do but no real reason to do anything if I don't feel like it. Who cares? No one-it is a sad realisation.

Grief

Waves of grief wash over me
drenching me with memories of you
Knowing we'll never meet again
Missing you in everything I do
All the things around me share a memory
of a time not so very long ago
When you and I made all our plans together
not knowing that your life would cease to flow
I call to you and wonder if you hear me
I try to feel your presence - but in vain
I miss you so very much my darling
My life will never be the same

I am still alright. I am not drowning in this grief but I feel lost and I cry more often. I don't like being on my own day and night. I need a friend. I need company. I need Brian. I could let my sadness overwhelm me but I will not. It would achieve nothing; it would not bring him back.

It is late but, as tired as I am, I will not sleep. So many things are happening; Clint, Dee and the kids are leaving to live up north and Julie flies to Taiwan tomorrow. I have moved to Perth after all this time and they will no longer be here. I will miss them terribly. Thank goodness Michelle and Mark are still near.

Haven't written for ages. Seems pointless somehow. I have been depressed and angry. I thought I had dealt with this, but I realise now that my anger was for Brian's pain, Brian's suffering, Brian's loss of life. This anger is for my pain, my suffering, and my loss of the love of my life. I am angry to be a widow at fifty-one. I am angry to be on my own and so lonely...

I cannot stop myself from looking at photos of Brian. They are tangible; it is as if I could reach out and touch him. But I can never touch him again. I wonder what will become of me. I don't seem to fit anywhere. I am one in a world made for two; everyone has a partner and I envy them.

My Darling

Hours turn into days, days into nights, tomorrows come, weeks turn into months, and memories pour in. I ache with needing you. Nothing can take away my pain. There are no words, no actions, and no promises that can ease the immeasurable sadness of losing you. You are entwined in my soul. Your voice echoes in my head with so many things I do and say, repetitions of all the things we once did together. It is strange doing them on my own. I walk the empty rooms hungry for the sight of you, the sound of you, the smell of you; all your clothes are clean and I cannot smell you anywhere. Your didgeridoos are here, my love. I can picture your head bent over them, painting late into the night; they are beautiful. You had such talent. I remember and I am so sad. I want you to come to me, somehow, maybe in a dream? I need you still. How are you? Are you happy? Will you wait for me? Can you hear me? I love you ...

I want to run away but where would I go? I miss Brian, I want him back; I am lost, I am lonely and I am frightened of what I will do with my life without his love to guide me. A part of me says, "you will be alright,"- and I almost believe it - but another part of me does not know what to do or which way to turn ...

We picked up Brian's ashes today; it was terrible to know that my beautiful man had been reduced to this. I was so upset I could not hold the container, but eventually I hugged it to me ... We made a tiny boat, placed the ashes within it, and sent it out to sea. I pictured Brian when he was strong, pulling his cray pots and casting his net onto the waves. It felt right to cast his ashes there, he is now as much a part of his beloved ocean, as the fish that swim within it ...

Always in my mind I'll see
Deep blue ocean - endless shifting sand
And you - my man of the sea
Thirty-seven years by my side - Forever in my heart

Freedom is new to me. Brian's illness and the ever-present fear of his impending death had condensed my existence to our home, the hospital, our family, and short excursions to the local shops. There is a big world out there. I am determined to get back into it and to put some meaning back into my life. I will be alright, if I let myself. I have emerged from the most tragic and painful experience of my life with a strength that I had not realised and a compassion for fellow humans that I had not previously known.

I must stop torturing myself by looking at photographs and crying over all I have lost. It hurts me and I have already suffered so much pain. I will continue to think of Brian often, but I must not deliberately dwell on my sadness. I have decided to attend a number of computer courses which, hopefully, will enable me to get back into the workforce. I am so glad that I have taken the step towards meeting people. It encourages me to get on with my life ...

I went to the Seminar again tonight and I am glad I did. People remembered me and came to chat. I loved the validation of me... It is far different than being with my parents, children or siblings. I met a woman who is deeply troubled. I told her of my experience and offered some coping tools. It felt good to reach out in this way. I hope I have helped her... I am grateful for my continued strength and ability to communicate with others. I am anxious to find challenge and fulfilment again and will endeavour to cast all negative thoughts from my mind. I will continue to grieve deeply for Brian but I rejoice in my life, my strength and my determination to move on...

I Want to Live

I want to live - I need to give

There's still love in my heart

And though you're gone - I must go on

Try to find a new start

I loved you long - I loved you true

No one can take the place of you

But I must try to shed some light

On the darkness of my life

Over a year has passed since Brian died - a year in which I have travelled a journey of sadness, healing, and self discovery. My experience has taught me not to take life for granted and to live each day with thanks for the wonderful gift that it is.

I have witnessed death and it frightens me. My awareness of the fragility of life, despite the strongest of wills, strengthens my determination to grab all that it offers me, with both hands.

For me, grieving did not begin on the day of Brian's death; it began on the day he was diagnosed. I mourned and existed in a state of total despair every day and every night for two years as I lived with the knowledge of his impending death.

I could not escape this torment even for a moment. I was losing my husband, my partner in life, the very core of my existence, the one person I had always turned to for love, understanding, and strength, and the one who had known and shared all of my hopes and dreams. In the most painful and harrowing time of my life I could not gain comfort or strength from the one person I needed more than anyone on earth.

There is no measure for such grief. I will always be proud of the strength and courage I found, despite this, which enabled me to ease Brian's journey. The knowledge that I was making a difference held me up even in my darkest hours.

There are many chapters in the book of life. Each chapter, once experienced, is not forgotten but stored in the heart forever. Brian is still with me and I see him often in the familiar characteristics and habits of our children. He is locked into a special part of my heart where no one can take him from me again. I think of him often but more often now I smile at the memories that are no longer of sickness and death; I remember the good times and give thanks for the many happy years we shared together.

EPILOGUE:

MY GIFT

It was a pleasant surprise when I received a call from Uwe; an old friend whose wife , Cheryl, had also passed away from cancer. She and I had worked together in Eneabba and were close friends. With Brian and Uwe we had spent many happy times, especially at the shack.

I had not seen Uwe since Cheryl's funeral five years past. It felt strange to be together without our partners and brought their memory closer to mind, but it was good to talk to him. My new awareness of what he had suffered, and his understanding of my grief, formed an immediate bond.

We reminisced about Eneabba, the shack, Brian's love of fishing, Cheryl, and the good times she and I had working in the Rehab. We were relaxed in each other's company and when he asked if I would like to see him again on his next week off, I said yes.

We saw each other several times over the following months and I began to look forward to his visits. I was still grieving deeply and when I needed someone to listen and to hold me when I cried, he was there. The ache that had so long been a part of me eased and I began to heal.

My Darling Brian

You are still within my heart - you will always be there - but I need to stop hurting. I want to be happy again. I must begin to let you go; I pray that you will understand. I need to be held, I need love to fill the void left by losing you. I have chosen to follow my heart; broken as it is, it is beginning to mend.

You cannot plan for love; it is something that happens, sometimes when you least expect it. This is true of Uwe and me. We came together as friends and our friendship transcended into love. Our love for each other is a gift and it came to us wrapped in hope. The greatest gift of all. Because without hope, life has no meaning.

Uwe

Just like rain after a drought
You held me up - thawed me out
Opened my heart - released the pain
Made me feel alive again
Gave me a reason to welcome each day
Anticipation now - not grey
More often now a smile breaks though
And all these things because of you
Our two hearts have been broken
We understand each other's pain
So special then is this chance
To learn to love again